Practical Dressage
for Amateur Trainers

Other books by Janice M. Ladendorf:
The Revolt in India, 1857-58

Practical Dressage
for Amateur Trainers

Janice M. Ladendorf

Photographs by Steven Murray
and drawings by Cele Schattauer

South Brunswick and New York: A. S. Barnes and Company
London: Thomas Yoseloff Ltd

A. S. Barnes and Co., Inc.
Cranbury, New Jersey 08512

Thomas Yoseloff Ltd
108 New Bond Street
London W1Y OQX, England

Library of Congress Cataloging in Publication Data

Ladendorf, Janice M
    Practical dressage for amateur trainers.

    Bibliography: p.
    1. Dressage. I. Title.
SF309.5.L3   636.1'08'86   73-149
ISBN 0-498-01285-9

PRINTED IN THE UNITED STATES OF AMERICA

Contents

Part V   HORSE MANAGEMENT THE EASY WAY

Part VI   PLANNING A TRAINING PROGRAM

Preface

Most works of nonfiction begin by expressing the author's appreciation for various kinds of assistance. This is one of the few traditions I intend to follow. Many people helped me at different stages. I particularly wish to thank seven of them. First, Mrs. Marianne Ludwig of Rochester, Minn. kindly went over some technical dressage points with me. Second, the linguistic analysis of the aids could not have been done without much advice, criticism, and encouragement from Prof. Howard Law, Univ. of Minn. Third, Prof. George Shapiro, Univ. of Minn., introduced me to the ideas which I applied in Part 5. Fourth, until I started working with Steve Murray, I did not realize what could be done with photographs. To get pictures that satisfied us both, Steve took almost 800 shots in 6 different sessions. His patience and cooperation were invaluable and far beyond what I expected. Fifth, my friend, Cele Schattauer, prepared the drawings for the book, modeled for some of the cross-country pictures, and criticized much of the final manuscript for me. Sixth, my friend, Dorothy Evers kindly typed the final manuscript for me. Finally, last but not least, I wish to thank my mother. She encouraged me at every stage and proofread many different drafts of the manuscript. She has also over the years listened patiently to many long monologues on the subject of horses. I do appreciate all this help. However, I take full and final responsibility for every controversial idea expressed in these pages.

Practical Dressage
for Amateur Trainers

PART I

Why Dressage

1
Who This Book Is For

In the U.S. today there is a rapidly increasing interest in dressage. This interest has by far outstripped the supply of competent instructors and judges. The ideal way to learn dressage is from an experienced teacher on a well-trained horse. Such horses are practically nonexistent. Since the typical amateur is rarely wealthy enough to purchase an imported horse or to pay an expert to train a horse for him, he is forced to consider doing his own schooling. It is for these inexperienced amateur trainers that this book has been written. It is especially meant for those who have no competent local instructors and must depend on occasional clinics and shows for guidance. Much of the material in this book should help illuminate the comments and criticisms passed out at these events.

A great deal of the current interest in dressage has been created by the competitive opportunities offered by dressage shows and combined training events. Despite this fact, this book is not specifically aimed at competitive riders, although they may find much of value in it. Correct dressage training can make any horse a better, safer, more comfortable ride. In particular, it can make him a far more enjoyable ride cross-country. Unfortunately dressage competition is just as artificial as any other type of showing. Consistent success demands a quality horse both in terms of conformation and breeding. Knowing the likes and dislikes of a particular judge and following all the current fashions are also helpful. However, the artificial values of the show world need not obscure the practical value of dressage. Correct dressage training should create a horse who will behave well in any circumstances. This is a quality that could not possibly be measured in a show arena. Those who still wish to show would do well to keep one axiom in mind: Compete not with other people, but with yourself to see how much you and your horse have improved.

Winning is unimportant compared to what you both should have learned from months of hard work.

Dressage can benefit any horse, but that does not mean everyone should attempt it. The first requirement for an embryonic trainer is seriousness of purpose. Unless you are willing to put in at least two to three years of hard, frustrating, exhausting work, leave dressage alone. It is far easier to do dressage wrong than it is to do it correctly. Misapplication of dressage principles, especially contact and collection, can ruin a good horse in a hurry. Dressage begins where most ordinary training leaves off. It is neither for children nor for beginners. The average child lacks the necessary patience and persistence. Even a serious adult needs at least a reasonably secure seat and some experience in handling horses.

The experts often maintain that you must be able to ride perfectly before you can attempt to train a horse. This is not true or I would never have succeeded myself. Good riding does help, but dressage schooling is one of the best methods I know for improving your horsemanship. Since this is a book on training, detailed discussions on position would be out of place. However, there are three aspects of riding that do affect success in training. The trainer should be relaxed, with the horse, and in a position to use his aids correctly. If the rider is not relaxed, the horse will not be relaxed and this will have a deleterious effect on his performance. A rider who is out of balance also handicaps his horse, but a rigid, perfect position may be more of a hindrance than a help. A rider's horsemanship should be judged by what he can do with a horse, not by how pretty he looks in the saddle. Getting good results from a horse depends on effective use of the aids. A good rider should be able to employ any combination of aids at any degree of pressure at any moment. However, working your horse on dressage is an extremely good way to learn to use your aids effectively.

What are the minimal requirements for dressage schooling? First, you need a horse. He can be any size, shape, breed, sex, or color, as long as he is at least four years old. Since dressage is extremely strenuous for a horse, your prospective pupil should be sound and healthy. Second, you should get copies of the current standards and tests. These do vary from country to country. The standards are a useful index to current definitions, while the tests can be a helpful guide in setting training objectives. The tests themselves are quite well designed, even though their interpretation may vary a great deal from judge to judge. Third, you will need a snaffle bridle, preferably

1. *These photographs introduce the real stars of this book. They are my two horses—Chief Reason and Gay Sprite. I bought them both when they were barely broken and schooled them myself up to third level. Neither was expensive, both responded well to training.*

1a. *If we can learn to do dressage, anyone can. Chief₁ is at a square halt on a loose rein and being ridden by the author. He is half-Thoroughbred, fourteen years old, and a 16.3 chestnut gelding.*

1b. *You don't need a Thoroughbred to do dressage. Gay is at a lively trot and being ridden by the author. She is half-Appaloosa, seven years old, and a 15.2 roan mare. She normally wears a drop noseband, Chief does not.*

with a drop noseband. Fourth, you need a schooling area that provides good footing for most of the year. It need not be the exact size required for competitions, although it should not be smaller. It doesn't even need to be fenced, as long as it has markers of some sort to enable you to ride precisely from one point to another. People did dressage for centuries before the size and markings of today's competitive arenas were established (see Fig. 1).

What is not essential for doing dressage is formal riding attire. As the protographs in this book demonstrate, I do not believe that clothes make a horseman. Personally I place comfort a long way ahead of mere fashion. I usually ride in jeans and a loose shirt because I have found from experience that these clothes are cheap, durable, and extremely comfortable. I also prefer jodhpurs to boots and breeches, mainly because jodhpur boots with straps give my bad ankle some much needed support. I possess one good pair of jodhpurs and a riding coat to wear on the rare occasions when I need something more formal than jeans. I prefer to spend my money on better care of my horses and lessons for myself, rather than on unnecessary clothes. What you wear riding is a matter of personal preference and convenience. You can wear a bikini for all I care; this has nothing to do with horsemanship. In my opinion, some of the most outmoded traditions in riding are the ones regarding clothes. To hear some people talk, you would think that it is impossible to school a horse unless you are wearing boots, breeches, gloves, hats, etc. As far as I am concerned, you do not need formal attire to enjoy doing dressage, any more than you need a quality horse.

There is a common misconception that dressage is only for an aristocratic elite. This approach to training need not be limited to those who can afford to pay for elegant Thoroughbreds, tailor-made clothes, and coaching from a European expert. In a very real sense, this book represents an attempt to separate truth from tradition. It strives to clarify basic principles for the practical rider who is interested in better horsemanship. For this reason it is not concerned with dressage beyond third level. After that point dressage can be regarded as an elite art; before that point it can be of value to anyone. On the other hand, if you ride merely for exercise, or to socialize with your friends, or for the shoddy glories of the show ring, you can stop reading right now. Dressage is not for you. It is essentially a solitary activity and its true rewards come from the increasing harmony between horse and rider.

This book has also been written for people who share my mania for asking why. Those who are fortunate enough to be able to work

Figure 1

The Conventional Dressage Arena (Small)

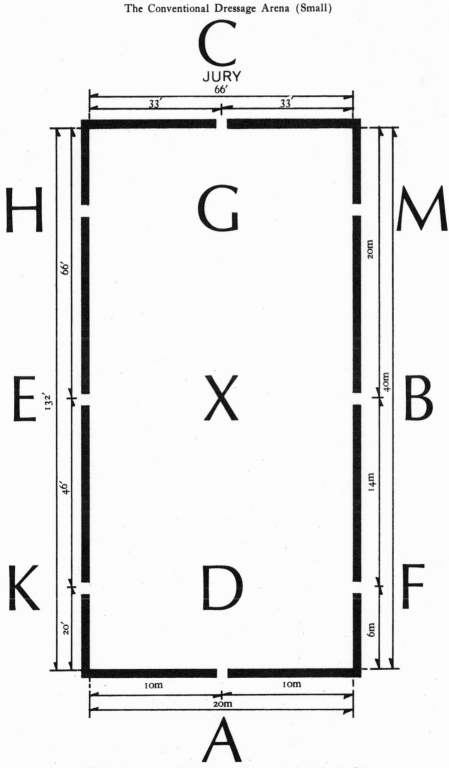

This is the arena used for competitions at the basic levels. It is
too small for much of the preliminary work with a young horse.

regularly with an expert may be able to ignore the theoretical side of training. The novice, working mainly alone, will find such considerations almost indispensable. The psychological and communicative aspects of training, as opposed to the physical, are particularly stressed. They provide the worst stumbling blocks to the novice, who has not trained four horses a day for three years. For some reason most experts like to argue that training can only be done by experts. The only way to learn to train is to do it, discovering and correcting mistakes as you go. Of course, the novice may take two or three times as long to reach the same goal, but most amateurs have more time than money.

2
What Dressage Is All About

Proponents of dressage frequently argue that it is the only way to train a horse. They are particularly fond of maintaining that dressage is a uniquely humane training method. This viewpoint is obvious nonsense. There are many legitimate methods. For example, the one Littauer has developed for hunters is both humane and effective. Many horses—hacks, hunters, jumpers, pleasure horses, cow ponies, etc.—fill their jobs quite satisfactorily without ever having received any dressage training. I have always liked Wynmalen's definition of dressage as the "art of improving one's horse beyond the stage of plain usefulness" (1952, p. 20). In other words, it is perfectly possible to get along without dressage, but many advantages accrue to those who do use it. I was once very skeptical about the practical value of dressage. Neither the grandiloquent claims of experts nor the horses I had seen in competition had impressed me. Schooling my own horses was what convinced me. Riding them has become a joy indescribable to the uninitiated.

What does dressage have that other training methods lack? There are three parts to dressage training—the physical, communicative, and psychological. Dressage does have physical and communicative techniques that are unique. Dressage can do much to improve a horse's physical capabilities. It can also greatly increase his mental capacity for understanding detailed and precise orders. However, the psychological approach aimed at obtaining willing obedience from the horse is not unique to dressage. Dressage techniques can be used either to obtain joyful service from a horse or they can turn him into a soulless automaton. The kindness or cruelty of a training program depend far more on the individual than on the method he uses. A true horseman strives ceaselessly to understand. His horse's opinions are much more important to him than those of other humans. Such people are just as rare among dressage riders as they are among other groups. Many of the early dressage texts are littered with barbaric schooling devices. People do dressage for many reasons—to obtain mastery over a brute, to prepare glorious spectacles, or to achieve fusion between horse and rider. A horse freely gives himself over—body, mind, and spirit—only to someone in whom he has absolute confidence and complete trust. The physical and communicative techniques of dressage can be of tremendous help in achieving this depth of understanding between horse and rider.

The gymnastic exercises that are the bases for dressage training can do many things for a horse. Most people do not realize how stiff, awkward, and unbalanced their horses actually are. A horse, who has become supple through dressage training, flows along with smooth, springy gaits. His active, lively trot is easier to sit than most horse's lazy jog. Such a horse is able to shift fluidly between the various degrees of collection, halting quickly and smoothly by shifting weight onto his hindquarters. He can readily adjust the length of his stride, covering cross-country the most possible ground with the least amount of effort. He is able to use himself more efficiently, flexing easily into turns, circles, and transitions. These results are gained through the exercises that increase the strength and flexibility of every muscle in the horse's body. This muscular development enhances the horse's appearance. It also increases his chances of staying sound and living a long, pain-free life.

The same exercises that were used to develop the horse's physical capabilities are also used to teach him an extremely efficient communication system. Despite their centuries of association, communication between horse and rider has usually remained on an amazingly primitive level. Most riders never progress much beyond a kick in the ribs to make the horse go and a jerk on the reins to make him stop or turn. Communication in dressage is smooth, quick, and practically effortless from the rider's point of view. The typical pleasure horse can be made to walk, jog, or lope in some vague direction. A dressage horse is expected to be able to shift easily between working, ordinary, collected, and extended paces. He can also be placed precisely down to the last foot. A really well-schooled horse responds to aids so subtle that they cannot be seen by a spectator. He almost seems to read his rider's mind, so easily does he carry out his desires. This communication system is also flexible enough to work well in any circumstances. The average hunter or cow pony may function quite

2. *The main objective of practical dressage is to make the horse a better cross-country ride. In the outdoor pictures, Gay is being ridden by our friend, Cele Schattauer. Cele has been taking Gay out once a week with Chief and me for about four months now. She says that she has never before ridden such a willing and responsive horse. This is a real tribute to the practical value of correct dressage.*

well in his particular job, but he would be lost in a strange situation or a new job. A dressage-trained horse should be extremely versatile. He can be quickly taught to do almost anything because his rider is able to explain a new task to him with such ease.

If the advantages described above sound attractive, then you may find dressage worthwhile. Unfortunately there is no way to learn dressage in ten easy lessons, no magic formula that can transform an untrained horse into a trained one. Even an expert usually takes about three years to reach third level with a green colt. Dressage training can be forced faster, but this usually results in an emotional or physical breakdown for the horse. Advancing one test level for one year's training is a realistic goal for the novice. It seems to take about two years of seemingly thankless effort before the neophyte really discovers what dressage is all about. Most people get discouraged and give up before they reach this point. Those who persist soon discover that a trainer's true rewards come from his horse's increasing ability and desire to please.

3

Training Objectives

The most striking part of a dressage test to a novice is its pattern. In preparing for a competition, he will spend many agonizing hours memorizing this pattern and striving to make his horse do the required movements or transitions at the appropriate letters. After all this effort, the usual results are remarkably low scores and a deluge of criticism. The point that the typical novice overlooks is that the required exercises are relatively unimportant in themselves. They are simply a means to an end. A test is designed to show the horse's progress in terms of a number of qualities which typify a well-trained horse. These qualities are listed in Table I. At this point, only preliminary definitions are given, as well as some indication as to where each quality is expected to appear in training.

The qualities in Table I are divided into three types—physical, communicative, and psychological. The physical ones will be discussed in more detail in Part 2, the communicative in Part 3, and the psychological in Part 5. This division is made only for explanatory purposes. Any time you are on a horse, you need to be concerned about all three types. Before you can get a correct response from the horse, he must be physically able to do what you ask. He also must clearly understand what it is you want him to do and consider your request to be a legitimate order. Keeping the appropriate balance among these requisite qualities is an essential part of training. Knowing which qualities to emphasize at which point in training for each individual horse is a real test of any trainer's skill and tact.

Table I, The Qualities of a Well-Trained Horse

Two terms will be use consistently throughout this book. Stage 1 refers to the first stage of training, Stage 2 to the second stage in training. This division is quite well recognized. A training level test is written for a horse in Stage 1, a first level test for one who has completed it. Riding a first level pattern is not particularly difficult; riding it well enough so that you and the horse can make the jump to second level is much more demanding. The second and third level tests have been written for a horse in Stage 2. For all practical purposes, a horse, who can consistently produce a good third-level test, can be called well trained.

Physical Qualities

Engagement of the hindquarters: This refers to the degree to which the horse is using the muscles in his back and hindquarters to drive himself forward. In Stage 1 this is expressed in the development of free forward movement at working gaits. In Stage 2 it is expressed in an increasing ability to collect and extend. This is the physical aspect of impulsion.

Suppleness: One of the major objectives of dressage is to develop to the utmost the strength and flexibility of every muscle in the horse's body. In Stage 1 a horse is not expected to show much suppleness, except for some lateral flexion on large circles. In Stage 2 the development of suppleness is of critical importance. Before a movement can be considered correct, every inch of the horse's body must be correctly flexed.

Regularity of paces: A horse in Stage 1 should show rhythm. He should settle into whatever pace his rider desires and keep to a relatively even tempo and approximately the same length of stride. A horse towards the end of Stage 2 should begin to develop cadence, which is absolutely accurate rhythm plus lots of impulsive energy. A horse with cadence appears to be swinging along with dancing steps.

The end result of the physical aspect of training is *lightness*. As the horse begins to develop this towards the end of Stage 2, he is able to shift his balance with ease, always moving with grace and energy.

Communicative Qualities

Obedience to the leg aids: This must be emphasized from the time the horse is first mounted. It is basic to the maintenance of forward motion, which is essential to keeping the horse under control. However, the horse does learn this obedience progressively. The farther along he is in training, the more effort does his work require. His willingness to exert this increasing effort is reflected in his obedience to the aids which demand it. This is the communicative and psychological aspect of impulsion.

Acceptance of contact: Anyone who isn't riding with loose reins can be said to have contact. In dressage this concept means something more. In Stage 1 the horse has to learn to stretch into the bit, establishing a light, live feel. Getting the horse on the bit in this sense is absolutely essential to the functioning of the dressage communication system. In Stage 1 the horse is expected to maintain contact while moving straight forward. He may still show some resistance in new work. By the end of Stage 2 the horse should remain reliably on the bit at all times.

Smoothness & precision of transitions: This reflects how well horse and rider are able to communicate. In Stage 1 smoothness is always to be preferred to precision. In Stage 2, as the horse becomes more supple and knowledgeable, his transitions should become increasingly fluid and precise.

Psychological Qualities

Relaxation: This is absolutely essential at any point in training. A horse, who is not physically relaxed, can never be supple. A horse, who is emotionally upset, is not capable of learning anything. Keeping the horse calm under the increasing demands of advanced training is always a problem.

Attentiveness: Before the dressage communication system can work effectively, the horse must learn to pay close attention to his rider. A green colt is very easily distracted by other horses and imaginary dangers. A horse also reflects lack of respect for his rider by lack of attentiveness. In Stage 1 orders are kept quite simple as the horse is learning to work on the bit. Before he can progress to Stage 2, the horse must learn to pay acute attention to a number of subtle cues.

Willingness: One of the major objectives of training is to get the horse to the point where he wants to obey. It seems to take about two years before a horse reaches the point where he is really willing to try and please his rider. The end result of the communicative and psychological aspects of training is

Responsiveness: The more responsive a horse is, the lighter and more subtle are the aids with which he can be controlled. It seems to take about three years before a horse begins to develop this quality. A really well-schooled horse can almost read his rider's mind.

For competitive purposes, the physical qualities are by far the most important. From the viewpoint of practical dressage, the communicative and psychological are of equal value. They tend to be underrated in competition because they are harder to see and most judges are looking for potential Grand Prix horses. Dressage training can do much to improve any horse's appearance and way of going, but few horses possess the potential brilliant gaits which are so desirable for high school dressage. These facts explain why I have divided impulsion into two parts. A horse with much natural impulsion can show quite a lot of engagement without actually working very hard. Another horse, less well endowed by nature, may have to exert a great deal of effort to attain even a minimum degree of engagement. So you need not be discouraged if your faithful steed doesn't score as highly as some flashy, disobedient Thoroughbred.

Although terminology varies, the value of the qualities shown in

Table I is generally agreed upon. What the experts disagree about is the relative importance of each quality. Each individual places the emphasis on different ones. This is the main reason why judges will so often score the same horse quite differently. The time indications in Table I and the tests are written for a nonexistent average horse. At a specific level a particular horse may be ahead in some qualities and behind in others. The intelligent trainer analyzes his prospective pupil, determines what qualities he lacks, and then concentrates on those exercises that will promote the missing qualities. The gymnastic exercises will be described in more detail in Part 4. Laying out a training program will be discussed in Part 6, along with the problems involved in evaluating a dressage performance.

Source Materials and Suggested Readings

This book is only intended to be an introduction to a discipline for which a lifetime is hardly enough to master. At the end of each section there will be a short discussion, indicating where the interested reader can go for further information. Complete citations will be given in Appendix A for all of the books mentioned in these discussions. The usefulness of the dressage tests and standards has already been mentioned. The American *Notes on Dressage* and the current tests can be obtained from the American Horse Show Ass'n, 527 Madison Ave., New York, N.Y. 10022. The material in this book is based on the 1971 tests and standards. The test requirements are summarized in Appendix B. The first chapters in Wynmalen's *Dressage* contain some brilliant discussion on the meaning of dressage. Young makes some pointed attacks on the artificial values of the show ring. For anyone unwilling to invest the time and effort required by dressage, Littauer's books describe an excellent training method. A number of subjects have been avoided in this book because they have been well covered elsewhere. Some of these topics are the history of dressage, conformation and breeds, stable management, the rider's position, lunging, and the breaking of young horses.

PART II

Producing an Equine Athlete

4

Laying a Good Foundation

The fact that the gymnastic exercises are only a means to an end cannot be overemphasized. The experts may mention that the cultivation of essential qualities is the ultimate objective of dressage, but they then spend most of their time discussing the gymnastic exercises. With this approach, it is no wonder that the typical novice thinks of dressage in terms of doing specific things. Indeed, some advanced riders never get over being exercise-happy. One of the most baffling problems that the novice encounters is dressage terminology. Descriptions of the gymnastic exercises are quite easy to find, as are dictionary definitions of qualities. Practically every textbook on riding has them, as well as *Notes on Dressage*. Unfortunately this type of information is more of a hindrance than a help to the novice. What he needs to know is the practical value of each quality or exercise, its place in an overall training program, and when a quality should be expected to appear or an exercise be used. Even more important, he needs to understand the complex interactions and causal relationships among the qualities and exercises. Filling this information gap is one of the main objectives of this book.

There are three major goals in the first stage of training (Stage 1). They are the cultivation of free forward movement, relaxation, and acceptance of the rider's aids. They all influence each other. The horse does not move forward unless he understands, accepts, and obeys the leg aids. He cannot be relaxed if he is fighting the bit. A tense horse cannot move freely; such tension is usually caused by resistance to the rider and his aids. Horse training would be simpler if you could concentrate on just one thing at a time; instead it is more like building a brick wall, a concrete foundation of basic elements must first be laid. The most critical element in this basic foundation is relaxation. The horse must be relaxed, mentally and physically, before he can be supple. Muscles that are tense cannot flex, bend, or stretch. A horse reflects resistance to his rider by stiffness throughout his entire body. The minute he relaxes his rider can sense it in the way he moves and feels. There are three common causes of resistance—fear, lack of understanding or confusion, and rebellion against the rider's authority. Fear and rebellion should be overcome as the horse learns to respect and trust his rider. Confusion gradually disappears as the horse learns first to accept and then to understand the aids. Trust, respect, and acceptance of the aids are goals for Stage 1; a detailed understanding of the language of the aids belongs to Stage 2. Once the goals for Stage 1 have been achieved, the trainer can then proceed to develop suppleness and full linguistic competence in Stage 2 by using all of the gymnastic exercises.

Since relaxation is so critically important, how do you get the horse to relax? First, he cannot be afraid of you or of being ridden. Consider the frightful shock a rider is to an unbroken colt. All of a sudden an awkward burden appears on his back. This burden interferes with his balance and issues mysterious orders in an unintelligible language. Most horses stiffen up out of fear at this point in their training and stay stiff for the rest of their working life. The trainer's first task is reassurance; he must convince his equine pupil that he isn't really a vampire in disguise. The more pleasant the horse's prior experience with humans has been, the easier this job will be. At the same time he is taking care not to frighten his pupil out of his wits, the trainer is also persuading the horse that being ridden involves moving forward. Once the horse accepts a rider without any fuss, and moves quietly forward on a slack rein at either a walk, trot, or canter, the first step in training is completed. The young horse can then be considered well broken.

After the horse accepts his rider without fear, the next step in training is to ride him energetically forward, aiming at developing free movement and rhythm. From the moment you first mount the horse, one principle is of paramount importance: It is imperative the horse learns that he must go forward when you apply leg pressure. This association must be almost burned in his brain. A horse who is not moving forward cannot be controlled. The origin of almost every disobedience begins with a refusal to obey the legs and go forward. This includes rearing, bucking, whirling, running out, nappiness, etc. You will discover how well you have taught your horse this principle when you first take him hacking or start teaching him to jump. Riding

3. The working trot in Stage 1.

3a. *Galatea is being ridden by her owner, Dr. Charlotte Hill. She is moving at an energetic working trot, typical of what a horse should be expected to show towards the end of Stage 1. The horse is still showing some resistance to contact with stiffness in her neck.*

3b. *Canadian Whiskey is being ridden by his owner, Pat Leatherdale. This horse is less advanced than the horse shown in 3a. He is accepting contact better, but showing less engagement.*

3c. Chief is showing correct contact at a working trot. He is very plainly driving forward into the bit. All the rest of the photographs in this book feature one or both of my two horses. Unless they are being deliberately ridden on a loose rein, they are always establishing correct contact. Unfortunately, it is impossible to specify what head carriage goes with correct contact. This depends on the horse's pace, stage of training, and conformation. Also, the main difference between correct contact (live, light) and incorrect contact (dead, hard) is a matter of feel and this cannot be shown in a photograph.

green colts is an exhausting task; it may take almost Herculean efforts simply to get them to move forward. At this point in training, the horse should be allowed to find his balance under a rider at working paces. He must be encouraged to find a pace at which he feels comfortable and then to keep to a definite rhythm. The horse has learned to move freely when he understands that he should always keep going forward at an even pace until he is given permission to change. Once his rider has set a pace for him, he should keep to it without any further pushing. When the horse moves easily and willingly into lively working paces, he is ready for further training.

As you are riding the horse energetically forward, you are also offering him the bit. This is one of the most critical, yet frequently misunderstood parts of training. Until the horse accepts both your leg aids and contact with the bit, you cannot communicate effectively with him. Few horses resent having the rider's legs resting gently against their sides. What most horses do resent is being asked to work energetically. Once the horse has thoroughly been taught to respect your leg aids, backed up when necessary by spurs or a whip, there is usually no further problem in getting him to go willingly forward. Accepting contact, however, remains a problem all through training. One of the defining characteristics of a well-trained horse is that he remains reliably on the bit at all times. This is extremely difficult to achieve. If the horse's reluctance to accept contact puzzles you, just consider how you feel in the dentist's chair. A horse's mouth is just as sensitive as yours. Anyone who attempts to force contact on the horse only creates resistance and stiffness because the horse is afraid of the pain in his mouth. Once a horse's mouth has been ruined by hard hands, severe bits, or forced contact, it may be almost impossible to get him to relax and move freely forward. If the horse is afraid of your hands, he cannot possibly be relaxed. As the horse is learning to respect your legs, he is also learning to trustfully establish contact with the bit. Until he does this consistently, no advanced training is possible. This is why the required movements in Stage 1 are so easy, the horse can only be expected to understand simple orders.

The key to remember about contact is that the horse must establish it, never the rider. Merely riding without loose or sloppy reins is not riding on contact as the term is used in dressage. Anyone who rides hunter seat has contact with the horse's mouth, but their horses are not necessarily on the bit. The contact they have may be light, but it is rarely live and elastic. When the rider forces this contact on the horse, it tends to destroy the sensitivity of his mouth, instead of cultivating it as a dressage trainer tries to do. When the horse establishes true contact, the rider will feel as though the bit has come alive in his hands. Getting the horse properly on the bit is based on driving him forward. As the rider pushes the horse into energetic, longer striding working paces, he should stretch towards the bit. Contact is established, not by shortening the reins and cramping the horse, but by encouraging him to stretch into a longer rein. He should initially encounter the bit somewhere way out in front of his knees.

The major goals of Stage 1 have now been described in some detail. By the end of Stage 1, the horse should have learned to obey the rider's legs and go forward, to relax under saddle, to work well into the bit, and to stay at a set pace. Unfortunately any one of these qualities can turn back into a problem. Overdoing collection or ring work can cause a horse to lose his impulse forward. A good training rule to follow is, "When in doubt, ride energetically forward." This

4. A good free walk, combining relaxation with energy.

can never be the wrong thing to do. Relaxation can also easily be lost again if the horse's training is rushed or forced. This quickly upsets the horse and his emotional reaction is reflected by tension in his body. Such tension usually results in hurried or irregular paces or in fighting the bit. Only a calm horse can move with rhythm. If at any moment the horse cannot shift easily into a good free walk, he has lost his relaxation. One of the dichotomous characteristics of dressage is its demand that relaxation must be united with movements which require more and more energy from the horse. A half-asleep or lazy horse may be calm, but he cannot be moving energetically. A well-trained dressage horse may be almost quivering with suppressed energy, yet he still must be perfectly calm and instantaneously responsive to his rider. A common mistake is to ask for more energetic movements than the horse can accept without becoming emotionally upset. This then leads to irregular paces and resisting the bit. Correct training must always be based on relaxation; unless the horse is emotionally calm, he will not be capable of learning anything.

So far the objectives of Stage 1 have been discussed rather generally. Within Stage 1, there are three distinct phases. First, a young horse has been properly broken when he calmly accepts being ridden and moves quietly forward at a specific gait. This is about as far as most pleasure horses ever get. In addition, a horse at training level is expected to show several more qualities. He should move willingly forward, establishing a fairly steady contact with the bit. He must be relaxed and keep to reasonably even paces. Occasional irregularities of pace or loss of contact should still be overlooked. Since the horse does not yet understand the aids very well, a certain amount of disobedience due to misunderstanding is also to be expected. As the horse learns to work consistently into the bit, these problems should gradually disappear. A horse at first level should be at the end of Stage 1. He is expected to move into lively, rhythmical working paces. He should be relaxed, work well into the bit, and calmly obey the simple orders he is given. He is expected to show that the proper physical, communicative, and psychological foundation for further training has been successfully laid.

5
Impulsion Through Suppleness

Once a good foundation has been laid in Stage 1, the trainer can then proceed to make full use of the gymnastic exercises in Stage 2. These exercises gradually develop the muscular suppleness of the horse's body, as well as teaching him to fully understand the language of the aids. Arguments over the naturalness or unnaturalness of these exercises are rather pointless. Any action which a horse can do must be an inborn ability or he would not be able to do it. This includes jumping and such circus tricks as running backwards. What dressage does is to select those actions which will develop the most desirable qualities. All of the required exercises are valuable aids in cultivating the essential physical and communicative capabilities of a well-trained horse. Each of these exercises will be described in detail in Part 4. The horse's ability to respond to the precise, complicated orders of advanced dressage is based on the development of both suppleness and linguistic understanding. In Stage 1 a young horse was given only simple orders and he was not expected to show much suppleness or accuracy. In Stage 2 all of the gymnastic exercises develop the horse's physical ability to respond fluidly and quickly to complex commands, as well as giving him the linguistic knowledge to understand such orders. If the trainer attempts to get fast, precise responses before the horse has developed the necessary suppleness and linguistic comprehension, the result will be rough, awkward, valueless movements and transitions. In dressage smoothness and less accuracy are always to be preferred to such rough, useless responses.

There are two basic types of gymnastic exercises: ones which develop longitudinal suppleness, such as transitions between gaits, and ones which develop lateral suppleness, such as circles. The linguistic principles that these exercises also cultivate will be described in Part 3.

In Stage 1 the horse was only expected to show a little of each kind of suppleness. Both began to develop only as the horse stretched into the bit. He did this only because his rider insisted that he move forward with more energy and a longer stride than he would normally use. A horse who is simply relaxed would step into his front hoofprints at a trot; a horse who is being energetically ridden forward at a lively working trot oversteps by one or two hoofprints. It is as he is stretching into this longer stride, that the horse reaches out and begins to look for contact with the bit. This is also the point at which he starts to develop longitudinal suppleness. In Stage 1 the horse was also expected to develop some lateral flexion on large circles. He begins to flex on circles only after he has learned to contact the bit. Since getting the horse to work on contact is one of the major goals in Stage 1, obviously he could be expected to show only a little suppleness towards the end of this stage of training.

In Stage 2 the development of suppleness is a major goal. Although the horse has been asked to change gaits and work on circles from the beginning of his training, these exercises do not have any gymnastic effect until he is working on contact. One of the first objectives of training is to get the horse to move straight, so that his hind feet always follow the same track as his forefeet. Since horses are naturally one-sided, just as people are right or left handed, this is not easily achieved. The rider has no way of getting the horse to move straight until he accepts the bit. Until he does this, he will wander around circles instead of flexing correctly. A horse whose hind feet are tracking his front feet on a circular track must flex. Contrary to what all the diagrams in the textbooks show, he is not bending his spine behind the withers. He only appears to do so as he stretches the muscles on his outside side and compresses the muscles on his inside side. This is what is meant by lateral flexion. The horse also has to apply more thrust with his inside hind leg to keep his balance. Naturally the smaller the circle, the more difficult this is for him. Flexion is a term which is frequently used in dressage. It is the horse's muscles that must flex as they are stretched or compressed in the various exercises. Flexion can also be incorrect if the horse is not flexing the right muscles. On a circle the horse would be incorrectly flexed if his head was pulled to the outside or if it were too far to the inside. In the first case he is flexed the wrong way; in the second, he is overflexing his head and neck to evade flexing the muscles over his ribs. Before an exercise can be considered correct, every inch of the horse's body must be properly flexed. When a horse is correctly bent on a circle, the rider feels almost as though the horse is wrapping himself around his inside leg. Before the horse will be able to move on a straight line and take an even contact on the bit, the muscles on his stiff side must be suppled up by working on circles. This is another one of the dichotomies of dressage; the horse must be worked on circles to enable him to go perfectly straight.

Transitions between gaits and paces are just as important as circular exercises. In Stage 1 the horse was not asked for any real collection and his transitions were too gradual to promote much longitudinal suppleness. Work at more collected gaits and less gradual transitions in Stage 2 will develop the suppleness in the muscles of the horse's hindquarters and back. This is what is meant by longitudinal suppleness. Pace or gait transitions again cannot be executed correctly until the horse is working well on contact. This can be illustrated by the transition into a halt. In Stage 1 the horse is brought to a halt by allowing his forward movement to gradually die away. In Stage 2 he is halted by a series of half halts which transfer more weight onto his hindquarters. If the horse is not on the bit when you try this, he will respond by attempting to halt on his forehand in a series of rough jolts. This is hard both on his legs and his rider. If a horse has been halted correctly, he should be able to spring right back into a trot or canter. He can push himself off easily only if he has correctly transferred part of his weight to his hindquarters. If he has been halted incorrectly with most of his weight on his forehand, he cannot step right back into a trot or a canter. The horse has already learned that leg pressure means forward, now he has to learn that it may also mean to shift more weight onto his hindquarters. To slow down or halt correctly, the rider must now use just as much leg pressure as he does when asking the horse to go forward. As he does this in a series of half halts, the horse responds by shifting his weight back and eventually coming to a correct halt. This is another of the dichotomies of dressage; the horse must be driven forward onto the bit by his rider's legs to slow down or halt correctly.

Both types of gymnastic exercises increase the horse's ability to engage his hindquarters. As he shifts weight back in transitions or in more collected gaits, he has to apply more thrust as his hind legs step under his body by using the muscles in his back and hindquarters. He uses these same muscles to push himself into more extended or faster gaits. As the strength and flexibility of these muscles are developed, the horse can then use or engage his hindquarters more effectively. Circular exercises also promote engagement since the horse has to apply additional thrust with his inside hind leg to keep his balance.

5a. The horse is flexing on a circle left. The extra thrust required from the horse's inside hind leg shows up very clearly. The ride is leaning too far to the inside. The horse is obtaining a beautiful flexion, despite his rider's imbalance. Possibly this accounts for his serious expression.

5b. The horse is on a circle right, showing lateral flexion from the opposite angle. The curve in his body, from tail to poll, shows up quite clearly.

6. *This series of pictures shows longitudinal flexion in two transitions—from a trot to a halt and from a halt directly into a canter.*

6a. *The transition begins at a trot. Gay is shown in the process of shifting more weight onto her hindquarters.*

6b. *The horse has changed into a walk and is almost at a halt. In both b. & c. the horse is well gathered together, showing a fair degree of longitudinal flexion. This flexion was developed out of a series of half halts, such as the one shown in a.*

6c. *A correct halt. The horse is balanced, standing squarely, ready to leap back into motion again.*

6d. *Springing directly from a halt into a canter. Gay is thrusting her whole body forward and upward into a canter. The strain on her hindquarters shows up quite clearly. The rider has made this transition more difficult for her by leaning forward.*

The horse is expected to show more and more engagement at each test level. This is the physical aspect of impulsion. As the horse develops the muscles in his back and hindquarters, he is able to apply more thrust or energy at any pace. Any increase in engagement is accompanied by an increased capacity for collection and extension. Within a gait a horse collects by shifting more weight onto his hindquarters and shortening his stride. He extends by pushing himself into a longer or more extended stride. Once the horse has developed the engagement necessary for more collected paces, this engagement is also expressed at less collected ones. For example, what would be a good degree of engagement at the working trot for a first level horse, would be a poor degree for the third level horse. In Stage 1 the required engagement is expressed in free forward movment; in Stage 2 it is expressed in the horse's increasing ability to collect and extend.

Engagement of the hindquarters then is based on a suppleness that is developed by use of the gymnastic exercises. From first level

7. *A schooled horse at a working trot. The rider is in the process of shortening the inside rein to re-establish even contact. Contrast this picture with photos 5a. and b. The pace is exactly the same, yet the more advanced horse gives a greater impression of power and lightness. The difference in head carriage and muscular development in the neck is particularly noticeable. The contrast between these photographs is a perfect example of the value of training. Before we started dressage, Chief looked much worse than either of these two green horses.*

8. *A collected trot. In contrast with photo 7, Chief is working much harder to obtain the increased degree of longitudinal flexion. The bend in his body is what gives the impression that the horse is closer to the ground. He is taking a much shorter step than in working paces, very markedly picking up his feet. The beautiful working trot shown in photo 7 was developed through the gymnastics required to achieve the collected pace.*

on, the horse is expected to show correct flexion in the required exercises. The more advanced the test, the more difficult are the exercises. The horse is also expected to show more engagement at each level. As a minimum requirement, he should show enough engagement to be able to execute the required paces and exercises. For example, to flex on smaller and smaller circles, the horse must be more and more collected. Of course, the more impulsion a horse can show the better, especially for competitive purposes. Unfortunately, a degree of engagement and collection that can be quite easy for one horse to attain may be very difficult for another. What distinguishes a potential high school horse from the average one is just this capacity for increased engagement. By the end of Stage 2 most horses have gone as far as they are physically able in this respect. This means that at the same point in training one horse may be able to show much more impulsion than another. To achieve the same degree of engagement some horses have to exert much more energy than others. Engagement represents a physical measure of how much muscular thrust the horse is actually using to drive himself forward. The horse's innate ability in this regard is limited by his conformation and natural gaits. Engagement is developed in response to the rider's leg aids. This response is a psychological measure of how much energy the horse is actually exerting in his efforts to reach the necessary level of engagement. A horse who has been poorly endowed by nature may have to exert extraordinary efforts to achieve minimum engagement. One with a real talent for dressage may have to exert relatively little effort to achieve a high degree of engagement.

From the practical viewpoint, suppleness and engagement are useful qualities for more than one reason. Even if a horse cannot achieve the type of brilliance that is so admired by dressage judges, the gymnastic exercises can do him a lot of good in other respects. A horse who has had this type of training is light on his feet in a sense that an untrained horse can never be. He is able to adjust his balance with ease, switching readily from one gait or pace to another. He can vary his degree of collection at will, a capability which enables him to make rapid, fluid transitions. He can flex easily into circles, turns, and corners. Even if his gaits lack a certain amount of brilliance, they are the best he can produce. He moves forward on a straight line, using as long a stride as is possible for him. All of these capabilities come in very handy in such activities as hunting, course jumping, and game playing. Working on the gymnastic exercises also teaches a horse the language of the aids and establishes a cooperative relationship between horse and rider.

6

A Delicate Equilibrium

From the physical viewpoint, the ultimate goal of dressage is the improvement of gait or the horse's appearance in motion. This end can be achieved only in cooperation with the communicative and psychological objectives of training. There are two aspects of gait—impulsion and regularity, both of which depend on a complex interaction of qualities. Impulsion grows out of engagement of the hindquarters and the horse's increasing willingness to put more and more effort into his work. Engagement is developed through suppleness by way of the gymnastic exercises. Unfortunately these exercises become gymnastic only if the horse is first relaxed and on the bit. Herein lies one of the major distinctions between classical and circus dressage. You can quite easily teach a horse to do many of the advanced dressage exercises in six months as tricks. Spectators then may be impressed with the horse's cleverness, but they will not be awestruck at the beauty of his lively, cadenced movements. These exercises will have a favorable effect on the horse's gaits only if the necessary relaxation and contact have previously been established. Regularity of gait depends just as heavily on relaxation and contact as impulsion does. A horse quickly reflects any emotional upset or resistance to the bit in hurried or irregular paces. This explains why a horse in Stage 1 is not expected to show a high degree of impulsion. If he does out of fear or nerves, it is usually at the expense of relaxation, contact, and regularity.

Keeping the horse calm and improving his contact with the bit are problems all through the horse's training. The importance of achieving relaxation and establishing contact in Stage 1 has already been well stressed. The major emotional problem in Stage 2 is usually confusion or misunderstanding. A horse who has been properly put to the aids in Stage 1 is no longer capable of disobedience. If he respects the leg aids and accepts contact with the bit, he has no way to evade responding to requests he understands. He finds these restraints tolerable only because he has learned to respect and trust his rider. In Stage 2 the horse is being introduced to more difficult exercises and to the full complexity of the language of the aids. At this point he can easily lose himself in a maze of unclear orders. This upsets any horse, especially one who is trying hard to please his rider. A confused horse, unless very tactfully handled, will quickly stiffen up and begin to fight the bit. This is why more difficult combinations and new work must be introduced so carefully to the horse.

For reasons which have already been described, contact also represents a continuing problem. One of the signs of a well-trained horse is that he remains reliably on the bit at all times. This is probably the hardest goal of all to reach in dressage. In Stage 1 the major struggle is to get the horse moving forward into the bit. In Stage 2 it is to keep the horse from losing this contact and fighting the bit when he is being given more complicated orders. There are two basic problems here. First, until the horse gains full linguistic comprehension, he is liable to become confused and resentful over receiving commands that he does not clearly understand. This reaction frequently results in attempts to evade contact. The second problem relates to the rider's attempts to gain more collection. To do this, he first uses his leg aids to ask the horse to go forward more energetically. This impulse forward is converted to increased engagement when the rider fixes his hands, telling the horse to collect, not to go faster. Learning to correctly coordinate the aids to achieve this is a real hurdle for most riders. Regardless of how tactfully and skillfully it is done, this process almost always upsets the horse into trying to escape the bit. At any point in training, if the rider tries to obtain more engagement or collection, he is almost bound to have trouble keeping the horse on correct contact. A well-schooled horse stays reliably on the bit because he understands and is willing to execute any order he is given. Until this time, he normally resents any attempts to get him to work harder at more collected gaits.

Any loss of relaxation or contact tends to have a bad effect on regularity of gait. There are three elements to gait, each of which must be regular or rhythmical. First, each gait—walk, trot, or canter —has its own sequence of footfalls or steps. Interference by the rider can throw these sequences out of order. One of the best ways to do this is forcing either collection or extension beyond the horse's current

9. Rhythm and cadence can be shown in any circumstances.

9a. Gay is moving at a working canter on a large circle. From this angle the lateral flexion shows mainly in the engagement of her inside hind leg and in the slight flexion of her head to the inside. To maintain regularity and balance on a circle the horse has to shorten some steps and lengthen others. The rider could be helping the horse by sitting down in the saddle.

9b. Climbing down hill requires an adjustment in balance if regularity is not to be lost.

capability. For example, forcing too much extension at a trot often results in forging; forcing too much collection at a canter can change it from a three-beat to a four-beat gait. Second, the horse's steps must continue to follow each other at exactly the same tempo. Keeping correct time is not as easy as it sounds. Moving at even paces is no more natural to a horse than is moving on a straight line. Third, the horse must also continue to use the same length of stride. When all of these factors remain the same, the horse is moving in regular paces. In Stage 1 a horse is expected to keep to reasonably regular gaits. In Stage 2, as the horse acquires more and more impulsion, he eventually achieves cadence. Cadence is absolutely accurate rhythm plus lots of impulsion. A really well-schooled horse dances along in perfect time, as though to music he alone could hear.

The rate of speed at which a horse covers ground is affected by two different sets of factors. The first is the conformation and size of the horse. The second is the three elements in pace regularity—gait, tempo, and stride length. The first set cannot be changed by training; bringing the second set under the rider's control is one of the objectives of dressage. Any riding horse should be able to change gaits. Even changing tempo within a gait is relatively easy. What is really difficult is getting the horse to change his length of stride without tempo alterations. The horse's ability to collect or extend in this fashion is developed out of engagement of the hindquarters. All of these factors can affect the speed at which the horse is actually traveling. One horse's collected canter may be slower than another horse's ordinary trot. Depending on his conformation, a horse's natural gaits can only be improved so far. However, regardless of the horse's physical limits, dressage training does give his rider absolute control over gait and pace. From the practical viewpoint, the important aspect of the gaits is not the brilliance achieved, but the control capabilities gained by the rider. What type of horse is thought to have ideal gaits is very much a matter of personal preference. Most dressage judges like Thoroughbreds, but a stocky, short-strided horse may be much more suitable for polo or cattle work.

Schooling a horse in dressage always involves maintaining a delicate balance among a complex set of qualities. Too much energy or impulsion without enough relaxation or obedience destroys rhythm or cadence. Too little energy, even in regular gaits, destroys brilliance and results in a dull performance. Both impulsion and cadence are based on increased engagement of the hindquarters, which is derived from suppling exercises. Unless the horse is both supple and relaxed, his impulsive energy and response to the aids cannot flow throughout his body. Without trust, confidence, and respect for his rider, the horse will not yield control over his body nor will he put enough effort into his work. Only increasing sophistication in the language of the aids enables a horse to understand the complex commands of advanced dressage. The more sensitive and responsive a horse becomes, the more difficult and delicate is the job of keeping this balance among qualities. Yet the better this balance is kept, the better will be the horse's performance. Maintaining this balance is based on the gradual development of perfect harmony between horse and rider.

7

Pace Control—Step by Step

The essence of dressage is to create in the horse the impulse to go forward and then to bring this impulse under control. Where many riders err, is in demanding more impulsion than they can easily control. A strong rider frequently forces the horse forward, then brings him back under control with rough hands. This may result in increased impulsion, but it excites the horse. A timid rider usually goes to the other extreme. He is afraid to let his horse go, so he chokes him with the reins. This also upsets the horse. Neither procedure results in correct movement. The problem in training is always to get more and more impulsion from the horse without any loss of emotional calmness and relaxation. One of the major goals in dressage is to give the rider the ability to collect his horse at will. This is difficult because collection is a state which the horse normally assumes only when he is excited or upset. To get the same change in physical balance from a calm horse takes a lot of training. Merely getting relaxation without collection is easy, so is getting collection without calmness. What is hard to obtain is a high degree of collection from a horse who is still relaxed enough to be supple and regular in his paces. To attain true lightness, a horse must be able to show all of these qualities at once. An untrained horse may collect naturally when he shies, but as he does so he loses his rhythm and evades his rider's control. Any horse can change his balance and adjust his paces with ease when he is running loose in the pasture. The objective in dressage is to bring these abilities under the rider's control.

There are many steps along the road to full control of the paces. The horse first has to find his balance and discover rhythm at energetic working paces. Then he has to learn to vary from the steady pace that he has mastered by shortening or lengthening his stride. Eventually he becomes supple enough to achieve the level of collection and extension called for in a third level test. Unfortunately the labels used to describe the required paces at the different test levels seem to vary from year to year. Regardless of what terms are used, the requirements for the horse do remain the same. As his training progresses, he is expected to develop more and more engagement of the hindquarters. As his ability to do this improves, so does the degree to which he can collect or extend. These abilities are expected to improve markedly with each rise in test level. This expectation remains, regardless of what terms are used to describe the required paces. For example, a horse is expected to show a much higher degree of engagement and collection at second level than at training level, even though both test levels currently call for working paces.

This problem of definitions has always been a difficult one in dressage. Each expert seems to have his own pet set of terminology. Certainly I hope the definitions I have been using are clear and logical, but this does not mean that other people necessarily use these words the same way. Until recently English has lacked an adequate vocabulary for dressage purposes. Indiscriminate translations from French and German have compounded the problem. Hopefully, some of the current confusion will eventually be resolved, but meanwhile people still have to carefully define their terms before they can discuss dressage. In regard to the paces, this difficult situation has been aggravated by the use of several kinds of misleading terms. First, many texts still attempt to separate working and collected paces by maintaining that one involves flexion of the jaw, the other flexion of the poll. I have never yet figured out how a horse is supposed to flex his jaw without opening his mouth. When he first comes on the bit, he flexes slightly in the poll. This is at working paces. As his education progresses, he eventually comes to flex his whole neck in a beautiful curve. This is at collected paces. Finally, just to confuse the issue, a trained horse always carries his head in a more flexed position than does an untrained one. In any case, quibbling about head position is rather pointless. A change in it is merely the final grace note to a pace change which is based on increased engagement of the hindquarters. Another set of texts attempts to define collection as an increase in the flexibility of the three joints in the horse's hind legs. Now these joints do flex more as the horse shifts more weight unto his hindquarters, but there is no way that the flexibility of a joint can be increased through dressage. What dressage gymnastics affect is the muscles which surround these joints. A horse's skeletal structure cannot be affected by training, his musculature can be.

10. *Pace control. On a schooled horse, the rider should be able to obtain any pace he desires. He should be able to set the horse's gait, tempo, length of stride, and degree of collection.*

10a. *The horse has stretched into a long striding extended canter. The pull on the muscles in his shoulder and hindquarters shows up quite clearly.*

10b. *A slow gallop. As compared to a., the horse is using as long a stride, but it has been gained by an increase in speed, rather than engagement. However, dressage gymnastics have helped the horse to gain this length of stride at a gallop.*

Now that the problem of definitions has been discussed, the next step is to describe how the different paces are developed through training. The first goal in working with a young horse is to achieve long striding working paces. At a working trot, the horse should be reaching under his body with his hind legs, overstepping his front feet by two to four hoofprints. Of course, a horse of good conformation does this naturally, but he finds it more difficult under a rider. It then requires a great deal more energy. Most nondressage riders do not insist on this type of engagement, the result is an overloaded forehand and eventually a lame horse. Most of the initial schooling at working paces is done at a trot. Before correct work at a canter can begin, the horse must be able to flex properly at a trot on large circles. This is essential preparation for cantering on correct leads. Also, working at a trot is usually easier for the horse since his natural gait is a gallop rather than a canter. It is generally less difficult to push a horse into an energetic working trot than it is to check him back into a correctly balanced canter. As he is learning to move into and stay at a working trot or canter, the horse is also discovering contact with the bit. At this point in his training he should not be asked to work on contact at a walk. There is no working walk, a free walk on a loose rein replaces it. From the dressage viewpoint the walk is the most dangerous gait. It has the least natural impulsion and the horse can all too easily get overflexed and behind the bit. This is why it receives so little emphasis in dressage tests. Almost all of the horse's schooling is done at a trot or canter; gymnastics at those gaits should eventually establish correct paces at a walk without any conscious effort on the trainer's part.

Since the engagement originally developed in working paces is completely expressed in forward motion, the initial working paces are not well suited to work in the dressage arena with its small size and constant turns. This is why much of the preliminary work with a young horse should be done outside of the ring or in an arena much larger than the standard dressage ring. As soon as the horse has learned to work on contact, the process of obtaining more balanced working paces for ring work should begin. These paces are based on increased engagement of the hindquarters. As more load is placed in his hindquarters, the horse should shorten his stride and decrease the tempo of his steps, achieving a more balanced pace. The increased engagement gained by this transition into a more collected pace can also be expressed in more extended paces. In this preliminary form of extension, the horse should be allowed to pick up the tempo of his steps as he extends. At this point in training the horse should be allowed to

10c. An extended canter.

10d. A collected canter. In comparison to the extended canter shown in 10c., the horse's body is more compressed and she is picking her feet up into a shorter, higher step. Her head carriage is perfect for a collected pace.

change tempo as he is changing his length of stride. This makes these transitions easier for him. As the horse's ability to engage his hind-quarters increases, he can be asked for more pronounced alterations in pace. The more advanced the horse, the more his transitions be-tween paces should be based on changes in stride length, rather than changes in tempo.

As he approaches third level, the horse should reach the point where he can be asked for full collection. As his working paces become more collected, the horse eventually achieves a pace at which his rider feels as though his front feet are hardly touching the ground. This is true collection. The horse dances along, taking short, high steps, arch-ing his neck into a lovely curve. Once this degree of collection has been achieved, obtaining true extension should be relatively easy. As more weight is transferred onto his hindquarters, the horse is increasingly able to extend by reaching out with his front legs, straight from the shoulder. Eventually the horse should be able to leap from collected paces into extended ones, changing in one stride from his shortest steps into his longest ones. When the horse can collect and extend in this fashion, he is also able to shift into ordinary paces. To obtain an ordinary pace, the rider simply lengthens his reins slightly, allowing the horse to stretch into a somewhat longer striding pace. His ordi-nary paces are between his collected and extended ones; his stride is longer than in collection and shorter than in extension. When the horse is able to shift effortlessly between working, collected, ordinary, and extended paces, he has achieved one of the major goals of dressage training. His rider should now be able to set the horse at any pace he desires, adapting easily to the demands of dressage, riding in com-pany, and jumping.

Obtaining complete control of the horse's paces may be one of the major aims of dressage, but it must be based on the prior development of many other qualities. Physically the horse has to be able to engage his hindquarters or he could neither collect nor work energetically. Without sufficient suppleness a horse could not radically alter his stride length nor his balance when he is handicapped by a rider. Before a rider can obtain pace alterations, the horse first has to learn to work at regular paces. None of these alterations would be possible if the horse had not gradually acquired mastery of the language of the aids. In Stage 1, it is difficult enough to get a horse on contact and to keep him at one even pace. Pace alterations can be developed in Stage 2 only through many endless hours of practice on the gymnastic exer-cises. Finally, the horse could not learn anything if he was not calm,

10e. *Gay is almost floating in this picture as she stretches into a beautiful extended trot. The reach in her shoulder and hip shows very plainly. To extend like this, a horse must be given enough rein so that he can also reach out with his head and neck.*

10f. *A collected trot. In contrast to the extension shown in 10e., the horse's body is more compressed and she is taking shorter, higher steps. She could be showing more flexion at the poll, but I believe collection is defined by the horse's body, not his head carriage. In my opinion, the amount of collection insisted on by many dressage riders can ruin a horse for cross-country work. My horses rarely give me the perfect collected head carriage shown in 10d., but they are not afraid to gallop and they work very readily on a loose rein.*

attentive to his rider's orders, and willing to obey. All of these qualities are essential to create a horse who is light, supple, flexible, and infinitely controllable.

Source Materials and Suggested Readings

By now the discussions in Part 2 should have helped clarify the test requirements and definitions in *Notes on Dressage*. The physical side of dressage has been the best covered in the literature. Most of the basic principles described here were pulled out of an intensive study by Wynmalen, Seunig, and Podhajsky. Readers who are interested in obtaining more information on suppleness, flexion, and conformation should struggle with Seunig. Those who are interested in gaits should look at Wynmalen's work.

PART III

The Language of the Aids

8

A Linguistic Reformation

The same exercises that are used to create an equine athlete are also used to teach the horse an understanding of a complex communication system. This system is one of the most puzzling and mysterious features of dressage, to spectator and rider alike. Experts may vehemently maintain that dressage is not merely teaching a horse tricks, but they seem to be unable to explain how teaching the dressage exercises is linguistically different from trick training. Anyone who learns to use the language of the aids soon discovers that this communication system is very different from the crude signals used in ordinary riding. It is uniquely complex in that it gives the rider very precise control over the horse's actions. It is uniquely flexible in that a horse who understands it can be told to carry out any possible combination of actions. It is uniquely generalizable in that it continues to function under any circumstances. All of these characteristics are true descriptions of what this system can do, but no one has yet found a detailed and adequate description of precisely how it works. Everyone who does dressage uses it, but the novice will search in vain for a clear description of how he is supposed to communicate with his horse.

To a critical mind there are many holes in the explanations that are usually given for how the rider's aids affect the horse. The ones that are couched in pseudo-mechanistic terms are especially ridiculous. This type of explanation defines and describes aids as though something the rider does could actually have an immediate physical effect on the horse. The novice is told that some aids will automatically drive the horse forward, while others will restrain him. A hand aid is supposed to have some inexplicable effect on the horse's opposing hind leg. Bracing the back pushes the horse forward. Shifting more weight onto one pelvic bone will free the horse's shoulder and force him to take the right lead. Any author or teacher who attempts to use such explanations has fallen into a treacherous logical trap. If you doubt this, just ask any of these people to define the precise physiological process by which these aids affect the horse. They can find no answer. No aid or set of aids could possibly have any sort of direct effect on the horse's muscles. Any instruction to the horse must travel through his nervous system. Any action by the rider acquires meaning for the horse only through patient instruction. Anyone who isn't convinced of this just has to try riding a really green colt. Something as simple as using both legs to ask the horse to go forward can bring about a number of reactions, including bucking, rearing, backing up, standing still, or sometimes moving forward. Those experts who use this mechanistic approach never seem to be able to explain why they cannot get on any horse and immediately obtain all the required dressage movements. After all, they are supposed to be based on actions which the horse naturally produces in the pasture.

The other popular explanation for how the aids work is based on the elegant and impractical premises of classical learning theory. Since the rider does do something and the horse responds, defining this action-reaction process as a conditioned reflex seems to be quite logical. Unfortunately there are two basic problems involved in applying this theory to dressage training. First, while it does explain trick training quite well, it is unable to handle the working complexities of the dressage communication system. The process of giving a clue, getting a specific trick, and giving a reward is exactly what circus trainers do use. However, this type of stimulus-response relationship has a tendency to fall apart outside of the circus arena or psychology laboratory. The dressage system continues to work under any circumstances. As a matter of fact, the meaning of a set of aids does vary rather fluidly with the situation, while a conditioned reflex is limited to only one context. Finally, unlike the dressage system, these conditioned reflexes cannot be used to express complex relationships among commands nor can already learned tricks be used to define new ones.

The other basic difficulty with this theory lies in locating an appropriate reward. Conditioned reflexes are usually established by using food as a reward or electric shock as a punishment. As Moyra Williams (1952) discovered, horses do not regard food as a reward and it is obviously impractical to import electrical apparatus into the schooling arena. Despite these facts, everyone still talks about reward and punishment in relation to the dressage communication system. Personally I fail to see how any normally applied aid could possibly give the horse either a pleasurable or painful sensation. The only reward which really works with a horse is stopping work for the day. This can only be used once in a schooling session, which is hardly enough to establish a number of conditioned reflexes. Of course, a rider may express general approval by petting his horse or giving him a brief break on a loose rein; but again this cannot possibly be done often enough. Even a simple dressage test requires six orders per minute, far too many to permit offering a reward for each correct response. Social approval or disapproval can be used with people, dogs, and to some extent with well-trained horses. Unfortunately no green horse ever sees any reason why he should have to work for a living. He may care a great deal about acceptance or rejection by other horses, but human praise or criticism leaves him cold.

If the conventional approaches are unsatisfactory, then how can the dressage communication system be explained? Attempts to define the aids in mechanistic terms or to locate a reward for every response get more and more complicated without ever arriving at an adequate explanation. Instead, the dressage communication system seems to fit into the pattern followed by human languages. Several authors have hinted at this linguistic approach. Podhajsky (1967) uses the term,

11. Treats may not motivate a horse to do anything, but they can help convince him that his trainer is a friend, not an unreasonable tyrant.

"the language of the aids," which I have borrowed as a title for this section. Wynmalen (1954) speaks of the aids as the ABCs of riding. Within its limits the dressage system does seem to function like a language. Of course, it does not begin to cover as extensive a territory as human language. It is limited to immediate directive action in the here and now. It does not operate at a very high level of abstraction and its time span is limited to the present. However, its structure is basically linguistic, not mechanistic.

The dressage system, like every other communication system, is built on an arbitrary base. Its signs, called aids, come to symbolize referents, or certain movements. These symbols acquire meaning only as they are patterned into conventional relationships. These conventional patterns must be learned by horse and rider alike. The horse first has to learn that the rider is using certain actions to communicate with him. What these actions are is immaterial. For example, Moyra Williams (1960) substituted touches on the horse's neck for the more usual aids and they worked just as well. The rider can use any action as a basis for communication. What gives the dressage system its uniqueness is the way in which its aids are structured into a complex system. It is its structure which makes a language something more than a mere collection of conditioned reflexes. The linguistic structure, which gives the dressage system its unique precision, flexibility, and generalizability, will be described in the next chapter.

One point cannot be emphasized enough. It is that this system must be learned. Most experts do admit that it must be taught to the horse, but they go on to talk about aids as though they could force the horse into certain responses. They are particularly prone to do this in discussing weight aids and bracing the back. How a rider sits on a horse does have a marked effect on his balance. However, no weight shift, which is unobtrusive enough to serve as an aid, could possibly have any forceful effect on the horse. This over emphasis on the supposedly automatic effect of the aids is partly responsible for much of the abuse which horses receive. Before correcting a horse, the rider should be sure that he clearly understood what it was he was supposed to do. This clarity is exactly what is lacking in most communication between horses and riders. Spending three years teaching a horse the fundamentals of the dressage communication system is well worth the results. Then the rider can communicate clearly and precisely with his horse.

One of the oddest features of the dressage system is that it is much easier to teach a new movement to a horse than it is to a rider.

This is because a rider has two sets of symbols to learn to the horse's one. He first has to learn to use the aids which tell the horse what to do. The horse also learns this set of aids, but he replies in a different set of symbols. Learning to interpret the correctness of the horse's response is one of the most difficult aspects of dressage riding. The dressage system encompasses both of these sets of symbols. The language of the aids can be described theoretically; the language of the horse's responses can be learned only by working with horses. Most experts do admit that even their supposedly automatic aids cannot turn a green colt into a trained horse overnight. Even if the aids did work automatically, this would not be possible because a young horse lacks the necessary suppleness. However, the same experts are puzzled by the fact that a novice usually gets such poor results from a trained horse. Anyone can ride a well-schooled horse, but his responses are not so automatic that anyone can obtain them. A novice generally lacks skill and sensitivity in using his aids, as well as the ability to interpret the horse's responses. Neither a horse nor a rider is able to communicate beyond the extent of his own knowledge. Both must learn to understand the dressage system by patient and persistent effort.

A green horse is in exactly the same position as a young child. He must learn both a communication system and acceptable behavior patterns from people with whom he has no language in common. Unfortunately for trainers, a horse cannot be physically dominated in the sense a child can nor is he motivated to need human approval the way that one human needs another. Given these facts, it is fortunate for us that horses are basically nonaggressive or we would never be able to train them. If an unbroken horse fights back, it is almost always out of fear. If a trainer cannot use force, social approval, or physical rewards and punishments to control a horse, what does he use? Control in dressage is based on the horse's understanding of the language of the aids, as well as the cultivation of certain psychological attitudes. The first step in getting the horse under control is to teach him to obey two basic rules of behavior. He must learn to go straight forward at whatever pace his rider sets until he is given permission to change. Breaking a colt involves teaching initial obedience to these rules, a process that requires considerable agility and ingenuity. Complete compliance with these rules, along with the acceptance of contact, is taught in Stage 1. In these preliminary stages, a colt should never be allowed to discover that it is possible to disobey an order. This requires a good understanding of equine motivation and character, a subject which will be discussed in Part 5. However, once a horse has accepted contact with the bit, he is no longer capable of deliberate disobedience. As the horse acquires more and more linguistic comprehension, his rider acquires more and more control over his actions. This learning process will be discussed in more detail in chapter 9.

In practice the dressage communication system works rather like a feedback control system. A typical communication segment has three distinctive steps. The horse is normally in a steady state; that is, he is going straight forward at a set pace. The rider changes this state whenever he asks the horse to carry out a gymnastic exercise. If the horse responds correctly to the aids, the rider stops communicating for a few moments. If the horse doesn't respond correctly, the rider speaks to him again, asking him to correct his response. This step can best be described as corrective feedback. When the horse has completed the desired movement, even if it was only a quarter volte, the rider then tells him to return to going straight forward again, either at the same or a different pace. This simple model explains the process of communication in dressage much better than the endless complications of the mechanistic or reward-punishment approach.

Using a feedback model has several major advantages. It explains why so much emphasis is placed on making the horse go forward in dressage. If the horse does not follow the two fundamental rules, the rider has no way to keep him under control. This is why dressage arenas are rectangular, not oval. In a rectangular arena the horse proceeds on straight lines and the rider is forced to ask him to flex into each corner, instead of merely allowing him to follow the rail around. The regular turns really make a horse pay attention to the aids. They also constantly reinforce his obedience to the two basic rules. Studying a dressage test shows the pervasiveness of the steady state concept. Each test contains sets of exercises written around two base gaits. They are usually a working trot or canter in the lower levels. After each exercise, the horse returns to going straight forward again at the base gait for a short interval. These intervals are usually the same as the breaks between individual scores. The feedback concept substitutes pauses or corrections for rewards or punishments. This avoids the necessity for finding specific rewards and for discussing punishment, except in those rare cases when the horse does deliberately disobey an order which he well understands. The feedback step is a critical part of training. The rider must know what constitutes an acceptable response from the horse and keep at him

12a. *The dressage communication system is built on the horse's adherence to two basic rules of behavior. He must learn to go straight forward at a set pace until his rider gives him permission to change. Here Chief is moving freely forward at a lively working trot. He is on a loose rein, obviously obeying both rules of his own free will.*

12b. *The rectangular shape of the dressage arena embeds obedience to these rules in the horse. Chief, now working on contact, is flexing through the corner. A trained horse makes such a turn only under orders.*

until he gets it. Eventually the horse discovers that it is easier to try and give the right response the first time around. Then his rider quits bothering him sooner. This costs him the least effort in the long run and enables him to achieve his major goal of leading the easiest possible life. An effective use of feedback is what enables a trainer to teach the horse the language of the aids. It also convinces a horse that obedience is the best policy. These goals are achieved through the years by means of many protracted and exhausting arguments.

9

Aids, Combinations, and Semantics

My criticism of the ways in which the dressage communication system is usually explained are not to be taken as criticisms of the system itself. The more I analyzed it, the more I realized how practical, flexible, and efficient it actually is. It is just that any communication system must be built on a foundation of arbitrary signs, which can acquire meaning only through conventional agreements. For example, most human languages are built around 40 to 60 bits of meaningless vocal sounds. These bits are called phonemes. Each language uses a different set of sounds, selected out of the extensive range of noises that the human vocal apparatus can produce. This is why spoken languages sound so different, one may be much more melodic or guttural than another. The human nonverbal communication system of body actions—facial expressions, gestures, and other movements—is just as variable. Even a human smile takes on a number of different meanings, depending on the cultural context in which it is used.

To communicate with a horse, a rider can select from quite a number of possible actions. In dressage this selection is limited by a rule which requires the use of invisible aids. This means that a rider must be able to communicate with his horse by making motions which even a knowledgeable spectator cannot see. This is a classic principle. Guerinere, for example, described secret aids in 1733 (*Dressage,* Sept. 1971, p. 7). Invisible aids can only be based on the use of contact. A dressage rider stays in constant touch with his horse through his lower legs and hands. His lower legs in their normal position rest lightly against the horse's sides. His hands in their normal position maintain contact with the horse's mouth through the bit and reins. To send the horse an order, the rider does not make any noticeable changes in his normal position. He simply alters the pressure levels of the continuous light contact that he maintains with the horse's mouth and sides. Such alterations are the arbitrary signs used in this communication system.

There are two behavioral rules that are absolutely essential to the functioning of the dressage communication system. They are that the horse must continue going straight forward at a set pace until he is given permission to change. When the horse is simply being allowed to follow these rules, the rider continues to maintain normal, light contact. When he wants the horse to change out of this steady state, he alters his normal light contact. He has two possible alternative actions which he can use with each of his hands or legs. He can either relax a hand, decreasing the normal pressure, or he can tense a hand, increasing the normal pressure. Normal leg pressure cannot be decreased, but it can be increased in one of two positions. For some reason which is beyond my understanding, these two positions are usually described as being on the girth or behind it. Since the horse obviously cannot feel any pressure which is applied on the saddle girth, I prefer to refer to them as Position 1 (P1) and Position 2 (P2). P1 is the normal one in which the rider's lower leg rests just behind the girth. P2 is 4 to 6 inches farther back. (See Fig. 2) Since neither of these two positions is related to any particular spot on the horse, P2 must always be established in reference to P1. This means that both legs cannot be used at once in P2; P2 cannot exist except in contrast to P1. Each of these actions—relaxing or tensing a hand, increasing leg pressure in P1 or P2—is an aid and is meaningless in itself. Its function in the dressage system is the same as that of a phoneme in human language.

Aids then are created by alterations in normal pressure levels. They can acquire meaning only in combination with each other. Just as contact is one of the fundamental principles in the dressage system, so is the requirement for combined aids. To issue an order to the horse, a dressage rider must use both his hands and legs. This is one of the most outstanding ways in which dressage differs from ordinary riding. Most riders kick the horse to tell him to go and jerk on the bit to make him stop or turn. This is never done in dressage. Even a simple turn requires the use of both hand and leg aids. These two principles—contact and combined aids—are what makes the dressage system into a language. They permit a rider to say a great deal to his horse in a very short time. This allows him to put complex combinations of aids together. This feature is what gives the dressage system its unique capabilities for precision, flexibility, and generalizability. A dressage rider can formulate very complicated orders. For example,

13. *The dressage communication system functions completely only when the horse is in contact with the bit. Here Chief is shown willingly establishing contact.*

13a. The rider begins to shorten rein at a free walk.

13b. The horse accepts contact.

Figure 2

Leg Position 1

Leg Position 2

a well-schooled dressage horse can not merely be told to trot, he can be told to execute a collected, ordinary, working, or extended trot. He can be told to pivot, back up, or sidestep a specified number of steps. The communicative methods used in ordinary riding do not begin to offer the rider these kinds of control options.

Table II shows the eight standard combinations of aids. As can be readily seen, each of these combinations can be utilized to give more than one basic command. This is another one of the unique features of the dressage system. In trick training one stimulus, whether it is simple or complex, can be associated with only one response. In the dressage system one stimulus or combination can take on many meanings. This is one of the many ways in which the dressage system re-resembles human language. Looking in a dictionary quickly reveals that any word can mean more than one thing. This is just as true of aid combinations. If the meaning of a combination can vary, then the system must contain ways to distinguish between otherwise similar commands. There are three basic types of clues which can be used for this purpose. They are the order in which the aids are applied, contrasting degrees of pressure, and the situational context in which the aids are used.

Table II, The Basic Combinations

Each of the combinations below can be used to give the horse three different types of orders: (1) To ask the horse for a change in state. In the ring this is usually a request for one of the standard gymnastic exercises. (2) To correct the horse for breaking or being about to break one of the three basic rules. These rules are that the horse must go straight forward (rule 1) at a set pace (rule 2) on contact (rule 3). In this type of correction, the meaning of a combination is usually different from what it is in type 1. (3) To tell the horse that he has misunderstood an order. In this type of correction, meaning remains the same as in the original command, even though pressure degrees may alter. Within a combination, there are three factors that can affect meaning—the order in which the aids are applied, pressure degrees, and situational context. The meaning of a command may be further refined by reduplication or its position in the sentence structure. The most general meanings associated with each combination are shown below. The semantic relationships among commands and the specific exercises will be discussed in Part 4. For each of the directive commands shown, it is assumed that the horse is in a steady state, following the three basic rules. Each of the corrective commands can be used to teach the horse to obey these rules, as well as to correct him when he breaks one of them.

Symbols — ○ Relaxing a hand
     * Tensing a hand
     L Applying leg pressure

These symbols will be used throughout the book to identify the combinations.

Combinations 1 and 2 are always used to govern pace.
Combination 1—L○○L   Combination 2—L**L

    C1

    C2

Commands: Change to a faster gait
Change to a faster or more extended pace
Go off contact
Corrections: Go forward (rule 1)
Stay at set pace (rule 2)

Commands: Change to a slower gait (includes halt)
Change to a slower or more collected pace
Rein-back
Establish contact
Corrections: Stay at a set pace (rule 2)
Stay on contact (rule 3)

Combinations 3 and 4, as commands are used for pivots or sidestepping, as corrections for controlling direction.

Combination 3A—L*O

Combination 3B—O*L

C3a

C3b

Commands: Pivot on forehand right
Leg yielding right
Corrections: As unilateral half halt to correct right twist (rule 1)

Commands: Pivot on forehand left
Leg yielding left
Corrections: As unilateral half halt to correct left twist (rule 1)

Combination 4A—L°* Combination 4B—*°L

C4a  C4b

Commands: Pivot on hindquarters right
Full pass right
Half pass (two-track-ing) right
Corrections: Don't change direction left (rule 1)

Commands: Pivot on hindquarters left
Full pass left
Half pass (two-track-ing) left
Corrections: Don't change direction right (rule 1)

In Combinations 3 and 4, the distinction between right and left is based on the direction to which the horse is moving.

Combination 5 is always used to obtain lateral flexion.

Combination 5A—L*oL
Left leg in Position 1, right leg in
   Position 2

Combination 5B—Lo*L
Left leg in Position 2, right leg in
   Position 1

C5a

C5b

Commands: Circle left
          Canter on left lead
          Shoulder-in left
          Counter canter on left
             lead
          Haunches-in or out—
             left flexion

Commands: Circle right
          Canter on right lead
          Shoulder-in right
          Counter canter on right
             lead
          Haunches-in or out—
             right flexion

In Combination 5, the distinction between left and right is based on the direction of the flexion, not the direction in which the horse is moving.

The rider must use both his hands and legs to communicate with the horse, but this does not mean that they should be used at the same time. For all practical purposes the rider normally changes pressure levels with both hands at the same time. This is also true of the leg aids. However, the hand and leg aids within a combination must never be applied at exactly the same moment. In some cases, the hands may be used first; in others, the legs. In dressage the leg aids are used to create the horse's impulse forward, the hand aids to direct it. Applying both types of aids simultaneously would be like using the accelerator and the brakes at the same time in a car. The result would be a complete loss of forward motion. While everyone agrees that the hand and leg aids must never be applied together, there is a good deal of disagreement over whether or not they should be allowed to overlap. One school of thought maintains that they should never overlap. This is probably the easiest policy for an inexperienced rider to follow. The other school of thought maintains that they may be allowed to overlap as long as they are never applied exactly at the same moment. Those who follow this policy argue that as long as the interval between initial application is distinct, overlapping should not confuse the horse. (See Fig. 3) This is the policy that I follow, but either one does work satisfactorily. What is important is that either the hand aids must precede the leg aids, or that the leg aids must precede the hand aids. These changes in application order are then one of the clues which can be used to distinguish among commands.

The next type of clue that can be used is contrasts in the pressure degrees at which the aids are applied. An aid can vary a great deal in its pressure. For example, a hand aid can be as light as a slight tightening of a finger or as severe as a tensing of the rider's whole arm. A leg aid can be as light as a mere tensing of the rider's calf muscle or as severe as a blow from a whip. As any experienced rider knows, some horses respond to much lighter aids than others. Aids that will provoke all sorts of energetic reactions from a well-schooled horse may not even be noticed by a less sensitive one. Generally the better trained a horse is, the lighter are the aids to which he will respond. However, this does not mean that two horses at the same point in training will be equally sensitive. A horse usually grows more sensitive through training, but there are many idiosyncratic differences in sensitivity among individual horses. Within the range of pressures to whch a horse is sensitive, slight variations in degrees of pressure can alter meaning. For example, if the horse is at a halt, the rider would use just a little more leg pressure if he wanted him to trot than if he wanted him to walk. These contrasts in pressure become more critical as the horse is introduced to increasingly complicated orders.

The third and final clue, that can be used to distinguish among otherwise similar commands, is the situational context in which an

Figure 3

Aid Sequences

Never use these:

HAND AIDS

LEG AIDS

Combination A   Combination B   Combination C

OK to use:

OVERLAPPING
AIDS
H = Hands
L = Legs

Combination A   Combination B

OK to use:

HAND AIDS

LEG AIDS

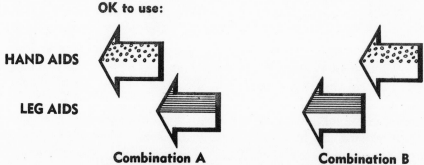

Combination A   Combination B

Although the hand and leg aids are used together, they must never
be applied at exactly the same moment. They may overlap as long
as one set of aids precedes the other.

order is given. Context is used in many ways in the dressage communication system. For example, what the horse is doing when a new command is given can materially affect its meaning. The commands for executing either the half pass or the full pass are an excellent example of the use of this clue. They are exactly the same except that the command for the half pass is given when the horse is in motion, the one for the full pass when he is at a halt. This is a relatively obvious use of context. The horse's skill in using context to anticipate his rider's orders grows with his experience. A trained horse has built up a whole repertoire of expectations. A young horse can be taken through a simple dressage test over and over again and he will not learn to recognize the repeated patterns of movements. A trained horse will recognize the command sequences in a much more complicated test after he has been taken through it only once. This is because he has learned to know the decision points involved in the various gymnastic exercises. He soon learns that there are some situations in which he will never be asked to do certain things. For example, he will never be asked to extend going into a corner. He also learns that some exercises contain certain alternative sets of actions. For example, when changing directions at a canter, he comes to expect an order to change leads, change gaits, or continue on a counter canter. The more experienced a horse is, the more ingenuity his rider must exercise in making full use of all the possible alternatives at such decision points. If he fails to do so, the horse soon falls into habitual patterns of actions, rather than responding correctly to the aids.

There are then several kinds of clues which can be used to distinguish among the commands associated with the same combination. Just how these principles are put into practice will be discussed in more detail in Part 4. However, these clues do not begin to exhaust the complexities of the dressage communication system. A combination is rarely used in isolation. Each combination, with the exception of C1 (L°°L), is usually extended by the use of reduplication. This means that all or part of the original combination may be repeated. Reduplication is used in human language to express the concepts of repetition or continuity. Its function in the dressage system is exactly the same. It is reduplication that allows a dressage rider to specify a certain number of steps in such exercises as backing up or pivoting. He simply repeats the appropriate aids to ask for each step. Repeating Combination 2 (L**L) in a series of half halts is what brings a dressage horse into a correct halt. In a circular exercise, the original aids may need to be repeated at intervals to tell the horse to continue on a circle. A young horse may even need to be told to continue his flexion at every step he is asked to take on a circular path. Reduplication is what gives the dressage system its unique capacity for formulating precise orders.

By using the appropriate combinations and reduplications of aids, a well-schooled dressage horse can be asked to execute any feasible action. He can also be asked to carry out any conceivable series of actions. Command can be added to command to any extent the rider desires. Each command sequence functions as a sentence within the dressage system (see Fig. 4). Some sample sentences are shown in Appendix C. There are three basic slots in a simple command sequence. First, there is the original command. If it is an order not to do something, it is usually preceded by some kind of hint that the horse is about to engage in undesirable behavior. If it is an order to do something, it may be preceded by the use of a half halt to call the horse to attention. Some authors and teachers do advocate this; I rarely bother. In my opinion, a properly trained horse should be attentive enough without any need for such special calls to attention. The second slot contains any reduplication of the original command that may be necessary. Other commands can be inserted here between slots 2 and 3. For example, in a serpentine, a new command plus reduplication must be added for each additional loop. Finally, the third slot contains an order for the horse to return to going straight forward at a set pace again. This order must finish every command sequence. It allows the horse to return to the steady state which the original command interrupted. Pauses, in which the horse simply follows these two behavioral rules, are what separate command sequences. Such

Figure 4 — SENTENCE STRUCTURE

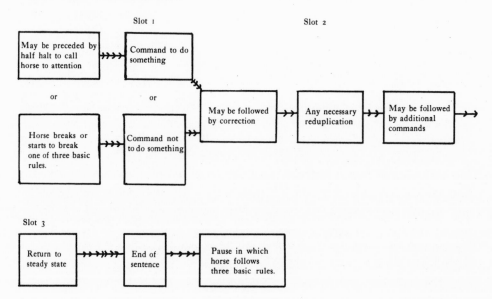

pauses in communication serve the same function as do periods in separating written sentences. They are also usually the dividing points between individual scores in a dressage test.

Sentence structure in dressage may be further complicated by the introduction of corrections. Slot 1 may be immediately followed by a correction if the horse has misunderstood the original order. Unfortunately errors are just as common in this communication system as in any other. Few horse and rider teams ever get through a test performance without making at least one mistake. Such errors can be caused by either horse or rider. Misunderstandings are even more common in schooling sessions. The only way in which a horse can learn to understand the complexities of this communication system is by making mistakes and being corrected for them. Such corrections should be made the second the horse begins to err in his response. If there is even a short interval, the horse will assume he has done the right thing. Corrections are usually expressed by the repetition of the original command. In such repetitions, the pressure level of the leg aids is usually raised slightly. This is another situation in which context affects meaning. By following a command, a correction does not change its definition, even though the pressure levels within it have changed. Such an alteration would affect the definition of an original command. A good rule to follow in making corrections, is to always accentuate the leg aids, never the hand aids. Accentuating the hand aids could quite easily frighten the horse into resisting contact with the bit. A distinction should also be made between explanatory corrections and punitive ones. Sharp or punitive corrections should be used very rarely. They are appropriate only when a trained horse has disobeyed an order that he well understands. Every allowance should be made for a young horse who knows very little, as well as for a more advanced horse who is being taught something new.

A command sequence in dressage can even be fitted into the conventional sentence pattern of subject, verb, and object. The command sequence itself, expressed through the medium of the aids, is the verbal action component. The subject is understood and unstated, as in most imperative sentences. It is, of course, the horse. The object of these directions is also unstated, because it is in the surrounding environment. Any thinking dressage rider must often have wondered why those letters are there in the dressage arena. They are one of the main features which gives the dressage system its generalizability into situations outside of the dressage arena. Whether or not the conventional markings, as shown in *Notes on Dressage,* are used is irrelevant. What is important is that any dressage rider gains a great deal of experience in making the horse do certain things in relationship to certain objects (letters) in the environment. A great deal of the conversation between horse and rider outside of the ring is concerned with other types of objects, which either attract or repel the horse. A normal horse want to follow other horses. He also prefers to avoid going through such hazards as mud or water. In such situations, C2 (L**L) can be used to say "Don't you dare follow that horse," C1 (L$^{\circ\circ}$L) to say "Go through that mud puddle." Working to achieve precise control over the horse can really pay off in situations outside of the dressage arena.

As has already been suggested, the dressage system is unique in its complexity, precision, flexibility, and generalizability. Its utilization of the principles of contact and combined aids gives it the capacity to formulate complex orders. The use of reduplication gives it the capacity to formulate precise, detailed orders. Its sentence structure gives it a great deal of flexibility. It permits the formulation of command sequences that can express the relationship—do this action, and that action, and—as far as is necessary. It can also express the relationship—I wanted you to do this action, not that action. The system acquires its capacity for generalizability by the way in which it uses situational context. The meaning of a command can vary, depending on what the horse was doing at the moment it was given, as well as what commands have preceded it. The relationship of a command to various objects in the environment can also affect its meaning. All of these capabilities of the dressage communication system do give it tremendous practical value.

10
The Road to Understanding

Now that the structure of the dressage communication system has been described, it should be obvious that a horse cannot learn to understand it overnight. Just as no baby is born speaking English, no horse is born with a knowledge of the language of the aids. A horse, when he is first mounted by a rider, is in the same position as a traveler, who has just arrived in a foreign country without speaking a word of the language. Neither horse nor traveler would have any way to understand what was being said to them in a language which they do not know. A horse learns as a colt to understand the language which horses use to communicate among themselves, but the dressage system is utterly foreign to him. He not only doesn't understand the language, he doesn't even know which of the rider's body actions is supposed to be carrying message for him. His problem is similar to the one faced by human scientists who are studying animal languages. Their first problem is to figure out what part of the animal's behavior is communicative. An extremely important part of the breaking process is explaining to the horse which of his rider's actions is being used to convey orders to him. Difficult as this may be, it is only that first step for the horse on the long road to full mastery of the language of the aids.

Once a young horse has been broken, his trainer can then proceed to lay the linguistic foundation for advanced training. In Stage 1 the horse must be thoroughly taught three basic principles which are absolutely essential to the correct functioning of the dressage communication system. They are to follow two basic rules of behavior and to accept contact with the bit. The horse first has to learn that he must move straight forward until he is given permission to turn. Second, he has to learn to keep to whatever pace his rider sets until he is given permission to change. The importance of teaching the horse to obey these two rules has already been well stressed. What has not yet been explained is how ridiculous these requirements look to an untrained horse. If you observe horses in freedom, you will soon notice two things. They change gaits whenever they feel like it and they never move in a straight line. It is hard enough to convince a horse that he should stay at one gait; convincing him that he should keep to absolutely regular paces is even a more difficult task. Moving on a straight line is just as alien to a horse as keeping to regular paces. The idea that a straight line is the shortest distance between two points is a concept which never occurs to a horse. He is interested in looking for the tastiest grass, not in covering ground efficiently. A trainer has to patiently and firmly convince his equine pupil that he really must obey these two rules when he is being ridden. Control over the horse's actions is always based on them. It is amazing how many supposedly well-trained horses have never learned these rules. The minute their rider either drops his reins or loses his balance, they either alter pace or change direction. If your horse does not go where you want, at the pace you want, he must learn to automatically follow these two rules before he can advance beyond Stage 1.

As the horse is learning to obey these rules, he is also learning to establish contact with the bit. In dressage all three of these principles are taught through the use of combined aids. As the rider's legs drive the horse straight forward, his hands are used to keep him from breaking pace. When the horse starts to stretch into energetic working paces, he also begins to look for contact with the bit. A trained horse should always be looking for this contact. This is why he stretches his head and neck first forward and then down when he is given a loose rein. He is following the bit to the ground. Until the horse has learned to look for and establish this contact, his rider cannot give him any but the most elementary orders. At this point in training, stimulus-response reflexes do explain fairly well what is going on. The horse cannot progress beyond such primitive communication until he has learned to work on the bit. Getting a young horse to this point normally takes about a year. However, this process can take longer, depending on the horse's age and temperament and his trainer's skill and experience.

Dealing with the unspoiled mouth of a young horse is relatively easy compared with remaking a ruined mouth. Once a horse has learned to fear and avoid the bit, straightening him out can present a real problem. There are a number of ways in which the horse can

14. *Following the bit to the ground. A trained horse should learn to look for contact with the bit. When released into a free walk, he should attempt to maintain this contact.*

14a. *The rider has started to let the reins go, but the horse has continued the contact by reaching forward and down towards the ground.*

14b. *Halfway to the ground and the horse has still kept in contact with the bit.*

14c. A loose rein at last. The horse's nose is close to the ground and she has finally received too much rein to maintain contact.

evade the bit. Young horses usually do try most of them out, but evasion should never be allowed to become a habit with them, as it so often is with spoiled horses. First, a horse can get above the bit by fretfully tossing his head or by sticking his nose up in the air, stiffening his back, and dragging his hind legs. (See Fig. 5c) Attempting to cure head tossing with a martingale often creates the second and much more serious type of resistance. Next, a horse can get behind the bit by overflexing and tucking his nose in towards his chest. (See Fig. 5b) This is usually one of the most horrendous consequences of forcing collection on the horse. Finally, a horse can simply lean on the bit, attempting to use it as a balancing prop or fifth leg. The answer to all of these evasions is basically the same. Ride the horse forward, pushing him into the bit with leg pressure. This principle explains why the horse must be taught to obey the leg aids before he can be asked to work on contact. It is his obedience to the leg aids which enables his trainer to persuade him to establish contact. Beyond this rule, there are really no set recipes for dealing with the various methods of evasion. Too much depends on each horse's personal reasons for trying to avoid contact.

Laying a foundation for teaching the horse the language of the

Figure 5

A. On the bit (collected).
B. Behind the bit. Any time the horse flexes his head behind the vertical, he is overflexed and behind the bit.
C. Above the bit. The horse frequently has his nose this far out in his less-collected paces, but this is combined with a less-upright neck position.

aids involves more than just getting him to accept contact and obey the two basic rules of behavior. There are five major steps which the horse must take on the road to full linguistic comprehension. The first milestone has already been passed in breaking when the horse learned which of his rider's actions were being used as aids. The second step belongs in Stage 1 where the horse is taught to associate each combination of aids with particular commands. The simple orders he can learn at this point in training are shown in Table III. With two exceptions he learns only one command per combination. This makes things must easier for him. The first exception is C3 (L*º, º*L), which is used to ask for both pivots on the forehand and leg yielding. Neither of these exercises is particularly valuable in itself. They are taught so that the horse will be able to understand the use of C3 (L*º, º*L) and C4 (Lº*, *ºL) as corrective aids. Both of these combinations are important in getting the horse to go straight. This will be discussed in more detail in Chapter 13. Since pivots are done only at a halt and leg yielding in motion, the horse usually doesn't have much trouble distinguishing between these two commands. The other exception is the one which usually causes problems. In addition to using C5 (Lº*L, L*ºL) to ask for circles, this combination is also used to ask for a canter on a specific lead. Learning to distinguish between these two commands represents quite a logical hurdle for a young horse. At this early point in training, he is not yet well prepared to handle such complex relationships among commands.

The third step towards linguistic comprehension comes early in Stage 2. The horse must now learn to differentiate among all of the commands which could possibly be associated with each combination. This is the point at which communication between horse and rider starts to resemble a language. The clues, which are used to accomplish this, have already been described. They are pressure degrees, the order in which the aids are applied, and situational context. The horse must learn to notice the slightest of contrasts in pressure. He has to learn to use order to distinguish among original commands and to understand reduplication. He must discover how the preceding commands can affect the meaning of corrections and additional commands. Finally, he has to learn the use of situational context. The meaning of a set of aids can vary depending on what has preceded their use and what the horse is doing at the moment at which they are given. The horse eventually should learn to anticipate both the most likely and the least likely orders in any set of circumstances. Conditions in the surrounding environment can also affect meaning. A horse learns to understand all of these clues, as he is mastering the many gymnastic exercises that belong in Stage 2. The orders he must learn are shown in Table III. The types of control, which his obedience to these orders gives his rider, are also described.

Before he can master the relationships between all of these clues and the meaning of orders, a horse has to have developed an adequate degree of attentiveness. A young horse is very easily distracted by the presence of other horses and various imaginary dangers. Before he can make the transition into Stage 2, he must learn to concentrate on his rider's actions and what they signify. Before a horse can become attentive, he must be relaxed so he can think and willing enough so that he is interested in obedience. The establishment of these necessary qualities is an essential part of Stage 1. Working on more advanced dressage requires a horse who is able to concentrate completely on his rider's orders. Even so, the horse is bound to make many mistakes before he figures out the dressage communication system. At this point in training, the horse may frequently be mentally confused. The important thing is that he remains emotionally calm so that he can continue to learn. His mistakes should not be allowed to upset either him or his rider. A trainer's job is to give clear orders to his equine pupil;

Table III, Time Scale for Commands

Exactly when a specific command is introduced to the horse depends on the trainer's discretion. In this table, C stands for Combination.

1ST STAGE OF TRAINING

Horse responds to crude, obvious (heavy) aids; his response tends to be slow, gradual (preferred to rough and abrupt), and imprecise.

I a. C1 ($L^{OO}L$) to go forward
   b. C2 ($L^{**}L$) to slow down and halt (used very gently to obtain gradual transitions)

II a. C5 ($L^{O*}L$, $L^{*O}L$) to turn (wide)
   b. C5   to circle (large)
   c. C5   to canter on a specific lead

III a. C3 (L^{*O}, $^{O*}L$) to pivot on forehand
   b. C3   for leg yielding

IV a. C1 and C2 to obtain slight changes of speed within a gait (introduced late in Stage 1 after horse has learned to stay at working paces).

Horse has learned:
1. To obey C1 and go forward in any circumstances.
2. To slow speed in response to C2 (Until the horse is working consistently on contact, he cannot be asked to respond to C2 by collecting. His transitions down are therefore rather slow and shift very little weight onto his hindquarters.).
3. To establish slight lateral flexion on large circles, in making wide turns, and in cantering on correctly.
4. To obey pressure of one leg in P1 (the leg signal in C3) to go sideways. This response is very useful in teaching the horse to go straight forward at all times until he is given permission to turn.

2ND STAGE OF TRAINING

By the end of this stage, the horse should respond to light, invisible aids, make smooth, fluid, yet rapid transitions, and work with a high degree of precision.

I Horse learns to respond to C2 ($L^{**}L$) by shifting weight back onto hindquarters.
As his ability to do this improves, he can
   a. Make more rapid transitions down
   b. Move at more collected paces
   c. Make wider variations in length of stride
   d. Flex into smaller circles

II a. C5 ($L^{O*}L$, $L^{*O}L$) is used to change leads through a walk
   b. C5   is used for alternate canter starts on a straight line in preparation for counter cantering

III a. C4 (L^{O*}, $^{*O}L$) to pivot on hindquarters at halt and walk
   b. C2   to rein-back from a halt
   c. C4   for full pass

IV a. C5   for shoulder-in at walk and trot
   b. C5   for counter canter
   c. C5   for haunches-in and out

    d. C4   for half pass

V   a. C5   to execute a volte at all gaits.

    b. C1 (L^{oo}L) and C2 to obtain major changes in length of stride and degree of collection without a change in gait.

Horse has learned:

1. Absolute obedience to C2 (collects easily)
2. Absolute obedience to C5—horse has developed high degree of lateral flexibility (voltes, shoulder-in, haunches-in and out), canters on and continues on either lead in any circumstances (counter cantering and canter starts perfected).
3. Absolute control over pace—horse can make rapid, fluid transition between gaits, length of stride, and degree of collection.
4. Absolute control of direction—horse can be placed precisely in any position by use of pivots and sidestepping.

the horse's job is to figure out what these orders mean and how to carry them out. A dressage rider has to concentrate just as hard as his horse. He has to be skillful enough at interpreting his horse's responses so that he can apply exactly the right aids at the right pressure at precisely the right moment.

The horse finally takes the last two steps on the long road to linguistic mastery late in Stage 2. As he is figuring out how to differentiate among commands, he is also gradually establishing a whole repertoire of expectations. He eventually is able to engage in some very intelligent anticipation as to what his rider is most likely to ask him to do in any given set of circumstances. These expectancies can relate to the structure of the dressage communication system. The horse finally learns that each combination is associated only with a certain class of orders. For example, C1 (L^{oo}L) is always used to ask for a faster or more extended pace. Establishing these relationships for all of the combinations is step 4 on the linguistic road to understanding. The fifth and final step is completed when the horse has figured out the general meaning which is attached to each of the hand or leg signals which are used to make up the combinations. For example, the leg signal (LL) always means, "More engagement of the hindquarters." These semantic relationships do give the dressage communication system another one of its unique features. A new command can be defined in relation to what the horse already knows. For example, counter cantering is based on the horse's previous knowledge of the aids for specific leads. All of these relationships will be discussed in more detail in Part 4. Once the horse has grasped them, he has attained linguistic competence. This process can take anywhere from three to five years. After this point the horse's vocabulary may continue to grow, but he already understands the basic structure of

15a. Before a horse can progress to Stage 2, he must learn to be attentive. Chief is sidestepping to his left, horse and rider leaning in perfect balance. Notice the alert, intelligent expression on his face. He is obviously concentrating on his work.

15b. Linguistic competence pays off. The rider has been able to place the horse in the best position for opening the gate.

the system. In a similar fashion a human child has usually mastered the phonemic and grammatical structure of his native tongue by age six.

As the horse's mastery of the language of the aids improves, so does his responsiveness. The more attentive and knowledgeable a horse is, the faster he is able to recognize and respond to an order. The more advanced a horse is in his training, the lighter and shorter are the aids with which he can be controlled. A young horse in Stage 1 tends to respond rather slowly to relatively rough aids. He is quite inconsistent in the amount of time it takes him to respond to an order. Since his rider is unable to anticipate his speed of response, they cannot be expected to show much accuracy. The better trained a horse is, the faster and more consistent will be his response to orders. This consistency enables a horse and rider team to show more and more accuracy. A well-schooled horse at the end of Stage 2 can almost read his master's mind. He understands a whole range of subtle clues and is frequently able to anticipate orders. He uses these skills to transform the slightest hints of his rider's desires into correct responses. This quality is one of the major goals of dressage training. It is based on the growth of the horse's understanding of the dressage system, as well as the development of relaxation, willingness, and attentiveness. A horse who has it is really a joy to ride.

Obviously developing this kind of responsiveness requires a great deal of time and patience. The horse first has to discover what actions the rider is using as aids, then he must learn to relate aid combinations and commands. Next, he has to discover and pay attention to many subtle clues which affect meaning. Finally, he has to grasp the general semantic relationships which tie combinations and signals to certain classes of orders. However, just because the linguistic structure of the language of the aids can be analyzed, this does not mean that a horse ever consciously figures out its phonemic, grammatical, or semantic relationships. He learns them unconsciously through experience, just as a young child learns to speak. Once a horse has learned these relationships, he does then respond to the aids more or less automatically. A trained horse does not have to stop and think about what a set of aids is supposed to mean, any more than you have to think about grammatical rules when you talk. His obedience, however, is based on understanding and habit, not on any automatic effects of the aids. Dressage training not only teaches the horse the language of the aids, it also engrains in him the habit of obeying those aids. For example, a dressage rider may use his legs more in one schooling session than an ordinary rider does in a year. Therefore, in an emergency his horse is much more likely to obey his leg aids than is one who has not had this type of training. Explaining to the horse what your aids are supposed to mean always comes first; this is followed by endless repetitions to establish the habit of obeying those aids.

One communication principle cannot be emphasized enough. This is that the language of the aids, like any other communication system, is built on an arbitrary base of symbols that must be learned by both horse and rider. What I have been describing is the system that I use myself, but there are other ways to communicate with a horse. What matters is not what actions are used as aids, but how these symbolic actions are structured into a system. Many different actions could be effectively used as a base for communicating with a horse. There are two common variations from the system which I have described. First, there are the five standard rein effects, which are found in many books on equitation. These are not the hand aids which I use, but I am sure that they would work just as well. Second, there are the weight aids, including bracing the back. These aids normally serve to accentuate the leg aids, adding another subtlety to the system. They may be very helpful to the high school rider, but I do not recommend them for the novice. An inexperienced dressage rider is rarely able to use them either correctly or effectively. The important thing is consistency, not which actions are used as aids. A rider must use the same aids to mean the same thing or the horse will never be able to figure out what he is supposed to do. What aids a rider chooses to use is unimportant just so long as both he and his horse know what they are. Just as a human needs time to acquire the skills which are necessary to communicate with a horse, so does a horse need time to learn to understand his rider's orders.

Source Materials and Suggested Readings

If any part of this book can be said to be a unique contribution to the literature on horsemanship, it is this one. To my knowledge no one has ever before analyzed the language of the aids according to linguistic principles. Until recently, this could not have been done, simply because we did not know enough about either language or communication. I spent about a year working out this analysis, under the direction of Prof. Howard Law, Dept. of Linguistics, University of Minnesota. I hope by doing so that I have brought our knowledge of communication between horse and rider up to date with modern communication science.

PART IV

Commands, Corrections and the Gymnastic Exercises

11

A Means to an End

The gymnastic exercises may be merely a means to an end, but that does not necessarily mean that they are unimportant in themselves. Each generation of horsemen has emphasized different exercises and quarreled about how each one should be correctly executed. The amount of communicative effort devoted to establishing and arguing over definitions is an indication of the importance of these exercises. However, no horse is going to obey any order until three conditions have been met. First, he must be physically able to obey it. Training always begins with the easiest exercises and finishes with the most difficult. In between, working to achieve the correct flexion in each exercise gradually develops the horse's physical suppleness and balance. Second, the horse must clearly understand what it is he is supposed to do. Each new exercise adds to the horse's knowledge of the language of the aids. Finally, the horse must be convinced that his rider's orders are both legitimate and safe to obey. The patient pursuit of perfection in each exercise teaches the horse the habit of obedience. Even given these three conditions, getting a horse to do something is never as easy as it might appear to be.

There are always two aspects to teaching a horse something new—reasonable demands and acceptable responses. Before a horse can be asked to obey an order, he must be properly prepared—physically, linguistically, and emotionally. One of the main values of dressage tests is they do give some expert guidance as to what should be expected from a horse at each stage in training. An order, which would easily bring an accurate response from an advanced horse, would only confuse or upset a young one. Adjusting your expectations to the horse's current level of competence is an essential part of training. Forcing a horse to do something for which he has not been properly prepared is usually disastrous, if only to the horse's confidence in his rider. If determining reasonable demands is hard, deciding what constitutes an acceptable response is even more difficult. A response that would be acceptable from an inexperienced horse would be unacceptable from a better trained one and call for a sharp correction. Gradually raising your requirements, in accordance with the horse's developing abilities, calls for a lot of knowledge and tact on the part of a trainer.

Normally there are three general phases in teaching a horse something new. First, the horse has to guess at a new meaning for an aid combination. Once he has figured out a new command, he then has to gradually develop the suppleness necessary to doing it well. Finally, the horse has to integrate his new talent into his existing repertoire, adding it to his semantic map of the language of the aids. In my experience, it seems to take about two years from the point at which a new exercise is introduced to the horse until he can be expected to do it consistently well. At any point in this process, feedback is critically important. Knowing when and how severely to correct a horse is what makes or breaks a trainer. Whenever a horse does not respond as well as he should, there may be many different factors involved. They may be physical in nature—from incipient lameness to stiff muscles. The horse may have simply misunderstood the order, been momentarily inattentive, or the original order may not have been given clearly enough. Every horse also has his off days and moments of rebellion. A trainer first has to figure out what caused the horse's unacceptable response and then apply the right remedy. This is where experience counts and most amateurs fail both in insight and patience.

Teaching a horse to well execute any of the gymnastic exercises demands a good deal of adaption to the individual. The exercises may be standardized, but neither people nor horses can be forced to fit into a rigid mold. Every horse encounters different problems in his training and progresses at a different rate. Every trainer emphasizes different qualities and exercises. For example, the psychological qualities that make a horse a pleasant ride are the most important to me and I simply love some exercises, such as serpentines. These individual differences lead to a different interpretative style for every horse and rider team. This is one of the main reasons why there is so much controversy over judges' opinions. In any art there is no one style that can be considered correct. There are bound to be differences both among individuals and different schools of thought. No one man, one school, or one generation can possibly have the final answer as to what is correct. Modern dressage is quite different in some respects from the dressage practiced in the seventeenth or eighteenth centuries. For example, today jumping is considered to be one of the basic gymnastic exercises, yet it is essentially a twentieth-century craze. Dressage now is often defended for its value in making any horse a comfortable ride cross-country, yet the ancient masters never ventured outside of a ring. Modern dressage should be regarded as multifaceted training, involving many kinds of activities. Certainly the qualities gained through working on the dressage exercises carry over both into jumping and cross-country work.

12
Combinations 1 and 2

Enough has now been said about general principles. The time to discuss specific exercises and aid combinations has arrived at last. The place to begin is obviously with Combination 1 (L°°L) and Combination 2 (L**L), both of which are used to govern pace. As commands, these combinations may be used to change gait, to change pace within a gait, and to establish or release the horse from contact. They are also used to reinforce two of the three basic rules that are essential to the functioning of the dressage communication system. These rules are that the horse should (1) be going straight forward (2) at a set pace (3) on contact. Combinations 1 and 2 can be used to correct the horse when he attempts to break out of a set pace or when he attempts to evade contact. An attempt to break one of these rules may be based on fear, lack of understanding, or on deliberate disobedience. The severity of the correction naturally depends on the horse's reasons for breaking the rule. As far as rule 1 is concerned, in using Combinations 1 and 2 the assumption is always made that the horse is moving on a straight line. These combinations are used to control pace. To obtain or correct an alteration in direction, other combinations must be used. They will be discussed in later chapters.

There is one more basic rule that has not yet been discussed. Unlike the others, this rule is so simple that it does not normally have to be explained to a horse. Rule 4 is that the more strongly an aid is applied, the more violently the horse is supposed to react. This relationship is so logical that a horse usually figures it out with very little trouble. However, applying this rule is not quite so simple for a rider. The problem is that some horses are naturally more responsive than others and all horses become more responsive with correct training. The first thing a rider has to discover on a strange horse is exactly how responsive he is. The horse will ignore aids that are too light for him to notice and overreact to ones that are too strong. Aids frequently must become rough and obvious before a young horse will recognize that an attempt is being made to communicate with him. On the other hand, the aids used with a well-schooled horse become invisible whispers, mere hints as to the rider's desires. Within a horse's range of responsiveness, slight variations in pressure levels do become very significant. However, an aid which represents a sharp correction for a responsive horse, may not even be noticed by an unresponsive one.

The application of rule 4 to Combinations 1 (L00L) and 2 (L**L) has some important consequences. This rule again is that the greater the aid pressure, the greater should be the reaction from the horse. If combinations 1 and 2 can be used only when the horse is going straight, then applying rule 4 means that the aids on either side of the horse's body must be used at exactly the same pressure levels. This means that the left and right hands must operate at the same level and so must the left and right legs. If these equal pressure levels are not maintained, then the horse will probably follow rule 4 and change direction. He will tend to turn to the right if the right aids are applied more strongly and to turn to the left if the left aids are applied more strongly. This principle explains why so many beginners in dressage have trouble obtaining straight transitions. They frequently apply their aids unevenly, the horse responds by making irregular and undesired changes in direction. All of the other combinations utilize unequal pressures to ask for direction changes. In Combinations 1 and 2, equal pressure levels must be maintained on both sides of the horse, if undesirable direction changes are to be avoided.

The fundamental importance of the movements which Combinations 1 (L°°L) and 2 (L**L) are used to control cannot possibly be overestimated. The value of getting the horse to work on contact and obtaining absolute control over his paces has already been well stressed. In Stage 1, the horse is taught both to work on contact and stay at a set pace. Part of this process is, of course, teaching the horse to work on or off contact without varying his pace. Once the horse has learned to obey the three basic rules, then he can be introduced to pace variations. There are three basic phases to teaching pace variations. First, the horse must be taught to stay at a set pace. Obviously before the horse can be asked to vary his pace, he must first learn to stay at a regular pace so he can have a base pace to vary from. Once he has learned to do this, then he can be introduced to mild variations in pace. This second phase usually begins late in Stage 1. Finally the horse eventually achieves true collection and extension. This requires quite a high degree of suppleness and engagement of the hindquarters. Because of this requirement, the third phase is usually reached only towards the end of Stage 2. Essentially corrections of unwanted pace changes form an important part of Stage 1, practicing deliberate pace changes occupies an increasingly important part of Stage 2.

Gait changes are just as important as pace changes and they too are obtained through Combinations 1 (L^{oo}L) and 2 (L**L). They are to the horseman what scales are to the musician. Their value is almost immeasurable. Obviously they must be part of both stages of training, but they are usually emphasized much more in Stage 2. Their role in promoting engagement of the hindquarters has already been discussed in Chapter 5. They are the fundamental collecting exercises. A horse cannot be directly asked for more collection until close to the end of his training. Up to that point, if the rider wants more collection, he simply puts the horse through a series of correct gait changes. Transitions into and out of a halt or rein-back are particularly helpful for this purpose. However, such transitions should not be overused until the horse has learned to go forward into the bit. Normally gait transitions are heavily used in Stage 2 and relatively little used in Stage 1. This is true only with young horses. A horse who has been ridden for years without correct schooling in dressage is usually down on his forehand. In this case, retraining such a horse usually involves using a lot of gait transitions at an early stage to shift more weight onto his hindquarters.

Combinations 1 (L^{oo}L) and 2 (L**L) are obviously rather closely related. First, they are both used to control similar movements and they both require equal side pressures if the horse is to continue going straight. Second, although their hand aids are different, the leg aids used in both combinations are the same. Whenever the rider applies both legs at equal pressures in P1, the horse is supposed to develop more engagement of the hindquarters. Whether this engagement is released into forward motion or converted into more collection depends on what the rider does with his hands. In both combinations the leg aids must be used first. The horse's response to these aids begins in his hindquarters, the extra energy gained travels through his body until it reaches the bit. At this point in Combination 1, the

16. Combination 1 put to good use.

16a. Forward into an extended canter. The rider is giving with the reins, allowing the horse to extend. This should have been done by lengthening the reins, not by slumping forward.

16b. Forward into a trot from a halt.

16c. Forward into crossing a ditch. As the rider tells the horse to go forward, she is obviously considering how best to tackle this obstacle.

rider's hands relax, lightening the normal contact and releasing this energy into forward motion. As the horse changes to a faster or more extended pace, he reestablishes normal contact with the bit. In Combination 2, the opposite reaction takes place. When this extra energy arrives at the bit, the rider's hands do not give. This means that the horse cannot go forward, so he shifts more weight onto his hindquarters and collects instead. As he gives in and flexes, the rein contact returns to normal. The increased tension on the reins in Combination 2 should always be due to the horse's response to the rider's leg action. The rider's hands never pull, they simply refuse to give in a bracing action. This action is usually referred to as using a fixed hand in the equestrian literature. In Combination 1, the rider's hands open the door for the horse, in Combination 2 they hold it shut against him. In both combinations the leg aids are used at equal pressures and so are the hand aids. The difference is that in Combination 1 the hand aids relax to the same degree and in Combination 2 they resist to the same degree.

However, as long as the aid pressures on the opposite sides of the horse are the same in Combinations 1 (L°°L) and 2 (L**L), then the leg or hand aids may be used at varying pressure levels. This is especially true of Combination 1. In it, relative pressures of the hand and leg aids can be used to establish the meaning of a command within a specific context. For example, if the horse is at a halt, the rider might want to ask him either to walk or trot. In both cases, the hand aids would relax to the same degree, but the rider would use more leg pressure if he wanted a trot than if he wanted a walk. This is true of all gait changes; the hand aids relax to the same degree, but the leg aids vary in pressure, depending on how extreme a change is wanted. The opposite situation occurs at a given pace when the rider wants to ask for either a faster gait or a more extended pace. In this situation, the leg aids might very well be applied at the same pressure, depending on how extreme a change is desired, but the hand aids would always differ. A gait change involves merely a momentary lightening of pressure, a pace change also involves lengthening the reins slightly so that the horse is able to extend. Giving a horse permission to go off contact is different again from any of these situations. To do this, the rider lets the reins slide through his hands, while using very light leg aids to let the horse know he isn't supposed to lose impulsion.

Obviously a young horse needs time to learn such a complicated series of commands. He has to gradually discover what the aid combinations at varying pressures are supposed to mean in a number of different contexts. The one thing which he must learn as soon as possible in Stage 1 is that C1 (L^{oo}L) means to go straight forward at once, whether it is into a faster gait, over a jump, or through a hazard such as water. The importance of imbedding this lesson in his mind has already been discussed in chapter 4. In normal circumstances, C1 should only have to be used once. At quite an early point in Stage 1, the horse should be expected to go straight into a trot or canter from a halt. He may need to take a few intervening steps, but he should respond immediately to one application of the aids. Once the rider has given the horse a command to go forward, he cannot afford to quibble with him about his obedience to it. Once the horse understands the meaning of this command, he should be corrected if he fails to respond to it immediately. Even with an unbroken colt, the first step in his training is to get him to go forward. At this point, the direction and speed are irrelevant, as long as he goes somewhere. After a young horse has learned to go forward in the ring and the rider has gained some control over his actions, then the next step is to teach him to go forward in the dangerous outside world, regardless of the circumstances. Teaching the horse this basic lesson is an extremely important part of Stage 1.

While Combination 1 (L°°L) should rarely need to be used more than once, the situation is very different with Combination 2 (L**L). Combination 2 is almost always reduplicated, Combination 1 practically never is. The process of reduplicating Combination 2 is usually referred to in the equestrian literature as using a series of half halts. Slowing down or halting correctly is basically much more difficult for a horse than springing off into a faster gait. Quick, smooth transitions up come early in a horse's training; quick, fluid transitions down are one of its end products. This means that Combination 2 is almost always used repetitively to obtain smooth gradual transitions. The amount of reduplication needed to obtain a desired change depends on two factors. First, the more extreme the change, the more repetition is needed. For example, to bring the horse down from a canter, more reduplication is needed to obtain a walk than a trot, and more reduplication yet is needed to obtain a halt. Second the amount of reduplication also depends on the degree to which the horse is collected when the order is given. For example, one or two half halts may bring the horse to a halt from a collected trot. The same horse may require 4 or 5 half halts to halt from a working trot. Of course, as more reduplication is needed, then more distance is also required to complete the transition. For example, a young horse may need 70 feet to halt from a working canter; while a schooled horse may need only 10 feet to halt from a collected canter.

Halting and the rein-back can also be considered as gait changes in dressage. They too are related to Combination 2 (L**L) and usually are obtained through reduplication. A correct halt should be relatively square, with the horse standing evenly on all four feet. Such a halt is a sign that the horse is responding properly to the aids and is working on the bit. A young horse should never be allowed to get into a habit of stopping any other way. Unlike the square halt, the rein-back is introduced to the horse at a much later point in training. It may be dangerous to encourage the horse to back up too soon. Dashing backwards can be a nasty way to evade orders and the horse should not be allowed to practice it until Stage 2. When the time to teach the horse this exercise finally arrives, the rider should use Combination 2 at a halt. The use of these aids ought to tell the horse that he isn't supposed to go forward, so he eventually should be able to figure out that he is supposed to go backwards instead. One or two awkward steps is all that should be expected from the horse at first and 4 or 5 steps is usually more than enough of this

17. A gradual transition down must be obtained through reduplication. This series of pictures shows a transition from a canter into a halt.

17a. Gay begins to flex back at a canter.

17b. On the verge of changing into a trot.

17c. A smooth switch into a trot.

*In a–c, the horse is on normal contact, flexing in response to the aids. In d. &
e. she has not yet begun to flex and has just increased the pressure on the reins
in response to the leg aids. This pressure increase has brought the bit farther
out of her mouth. In d. & e., a half halt is being applied; and a.–c., the horse
is slowing down between half halts.*

17d. A half halt at a trot.

17e. Half halting again to push the horse into a square halt.

exercise. Combination 2 is usually repeated to call for each step and the last step should always be followed by a command to go forward. Both of these policies help keep this movement under the rider's control.

So far reduplication has been described as the only means of varying the commands associated with Combination 2 (L**L), but pressure variations can also be used to affect meaning. Unlike most of the pressure contrasts used in Combination 1 (L°°L), the contrasts in Combination 2 are usually between whole combinations rather than between the aids within a combination. All of these pressure contrasts are, of course, based on the application of rule 4. There are three basic levels at which Combination 2 is normally used. The highest or heaviest is used for the half halts which control gait changes. Somewhat lighter are the half halts used to obtain more collected paces or to ask the horse to establish contact. Both of these commands usually involve reduplication. The difference between them is one of context. The horse can only be asked to collect if he is already on contact and he can establish contact only from a loose rein. To ask the horse to go on contact, the rider uses a series of moderate leg aids as he gradually shortens reins and repeatedly fixes his hands. The lightest use of Combination 2 is the half halt which is

17f. Combination 2 is also used to obtain a rein-back from a halt. The rider is in the process of reduplicating Combination 2 to ask the horse to continue the movement with another step. A horse is supposed to back one long step at a time, alternating diagonal pairs of legs, just as he moves forward at a trot. However, this is a very difficult gymnastic exercise, so the horse· first moves backwards one foot at a time, taking short steps. Gay here is backing correctly.

used to call the horse to attention and warn him that a command is coming. Such calls are the only commands in Combination 2 for which no reduplication is regularly used.

Combinations 1 (L°°L) and 2 (L**L) also play several important roles as major corrections. Their first role is to teach the horse to obey rule 2, which is to stay at a set pace. From the linguistic point of view, the only difference between a correction which enforces rule 2 and an order to change pace is one of context. A correction follows the horse's attempt to break out of a set pace, an order precedes such a pace change. If the horse breaks into a faster pace, the rider normally corrects him by using Combination 2 just as he would to ask the horse to collect. If the horse breaks into a slower pace, the rider corrects him by using Combination 1 just as he would to ask the horse to extend. The pressure levels of the aids used does, however, vary a good deal with the individual situation. In a correction, it would depend on the horse's stage of training and how bad the break was. For example, a young horse, who does not yet understand rule 2, should be corrected much more gently than one who knows better. Also, stronger aids would be used for correcting a major break, such as a change in gait, than for a minor change in pace. The pressure levels of the aids used in an order will also vary, depending on how extreme a pace change the rider wants and the horse's current capabilities. The horse's ability to collect or extend depends very much on the degree to which he can engage his hindquarters and this improves with training. There is never any point in demanding more from a horse than he is physically capable of doing. Whether for ordering a pace change or correcting one, the main point to remember is that Combination 1 is used to ask for more speed, Combination 2 for less.

The second major corrective role which Combinations 1 (L°°L) and 2 (L**L) can play relates to rule 3, which is to stay on contact. Combination 1, of course, is used to give the horse some much needed relief from working on the bit. Combination 2 is used when the horse attempts to evade contact. There really are no set rules for applying Combination 2 in evasion attempts. Too much depends on the specific situation and the horse's reasons for resistance. However, one general principle does work in most cases. This is to combine very strong leg aids with light hand aids. Most evasions are basically refusals to go forward into the bit and strengthening the leg aids is the obvious means of correcting this. It is always the leg aids which should be accentuated in any corrective use of Combination 1 or 2. This is true whether the correction is for breaking one of the basic rules, disobeying a specific order, or for clearing up a misunderstanding. The hand aids used in Combination 1 cannot, of course, become punishing since they represent a giving action. The ones used with Combination 2 can be, but their use at a punishing or painful level should be rare indeed. Most riders spend far too much time hauling or jerking on the horse's mouth. Such overuse of the hand aids is an excellent way to convince the horse that he should make every effort to avoid working properly into the bit.

This discussion of the commands, corrections, and exercises which are semantically related to Combinations 1 (L°°L) and 2 (L**L) is now complete. Since there are no magic formulas for getting the horse to respond correctly, I have simply tried to describe some general principles and logical relationships. No one could possibly prescribe the right aids, in the right order, at the right pressure levels to fit any and all situations. A rider must always use his experience and knowledge as a guide in figuring out exactly what to do. Many factors affect the aids which should be used in specific circumstances. Much depends on the individual horse's conformation, temperament, and stage of training. A good deal also depends on the rider's level of skill. Even more may depend on specific characteristics of the situation, such as the presence of other horses. All a theoretical analysis can hope to do is help the reader learn some basic principles which he can apply to working with his own horse.

13

Combinations 3 and 4

Like Combinations 1 (L°°L) and 2 (L**L), Combinations 3 (L*°, °*L) and 4 (L°*, *°L) are similar, yet different. They do control similar movements and are based on the same aids. As commands, they are used to ask for pivots and sidestepping; as corrections, they are used to teach the horse to go straight forward (rule 1). Any time the horse breaks this rule, Combination 3 or 4 is used to correct him. In using Combinations 1 and 2, the assumption was made that the horse was going straight forward. In Combinations 3 and 4, a change of direction is always involved, whether the horse is responding to an order or being corrected for breaking rule 1. For these combinations the assumption is always made that the horse is staying at a set pace (rule 2) on contact (rule 3). If he breaks either of these rules during an exercise related to Combination 3 or 4, then Combination 1 or 2 must be used to correct him. Since Combinations 3 and 4 always involve direction changes, they do have to be partially based on unequal aid pressures. They also need two variants, A or B, depending on whether the change is to the right or left. As Table II shows, Combinations 3 and 4 are based on the same hand and leg aids. The only difference between them is that in Combination 3, the rider's active leg and tense hand are on the same side of the horse; in Combination 4, they are on opposite sides. Since the relationship between the hand and leg aids in Combination 3 is much easier for the horse to understand, the movements associated with it are taught in Stage 1. Since Combination 4 is more difficult, the movements associated with it are taught to the horse in Stage 2.

As Table II shows, the same hand aids are used in Combination 3 (L*°, °*L), 4 (L°*, *°L), and 5 (L°*L, L*°L). In all six combinations, one hand is tense, the other relaxed. The differences between the combinations are, of course, based on the way in which they are combined with the leg aids. In Combinations 1 and 2, the horse was always going forward and looking straight ahead. (Position straight) In all of the other combinations, he is looking either to the right (Position Right) or to the left (Position Left). In Position Straight, both of the rider's hands must either relax or tense. Otherwise, the horse's head position would alter and he would tend to change direction. To obtain either Position Right or Left, the rider simply relaxes one hand and tenses the other. If he tenses the right hand, the horse is supposed to switch to Position Right. If he tenses the left hand, the horse is supposed to switch to Position Left. In applying these aids, it is extremely important to apply them at equal pressures. One hand must relax to the same extent that the other one gives. This process usually involves some readjustment in rein lengths. In using his hand aids, the rider must always maintain an even contact with the horse's mouth. If he fails to do this, the horse may well be provoked into resisting contact. Combinations 3, 4, and 5 do utilize unequal pressures, but these pressures are reflected only in the leg aids, never in the hand aids.

Obviously all these different positions are something which the horse has to learn gradually. The first thing he must learn in Stage 1 is to go forward into the bit in Position Straight. While he is still learning to work on contact, he is usually asked to assume Position Right or Left only as part of an aid combination. After he has learned to obey the three basic rules, he then can be allowed to practice assuming either Position Right or Left, as he is moving forward on a straight line. This involves using C3A (L*o) to obtain Position Left and C3B (o*L) to obtain Position Right. In both sets of aids, the pressure levels of the hand aids depend on the degree of change desired and the leg aids are used rather lightly. Once the meaning of these two positions has been explained to the horse, then he can be taught to always flex to the inside as he moves around a ring. Going to the right or clockwise, he should assume Position Right. Going to the left or counterclockwise, he should assume Position Left. The horse is usually taught to do this fairly early in Stage 2. Once the horse has learned to maintain these positions, the rider's hand aids can become more and more unobtrusive. Instead of putting the horse into position as part of a command, the rider may just need to slightly alter an already existing position. Of course, then any time the horse is asked to change direction, the rider also has to readjust his reins and ask the horse to switch to the opposite position. In changing positions, the horse naturally has to pass through Position Straight. This is the point at which he can also be asked to alter gaits. Normally any gait change should be executed when the horse is in Position Straight.

Now that the hand aids have been defined, the next step is to discuss specific movements. There are two basic exercises which are associated with Combination 3 (L*°, °*L). They are the pivot on the forehand and leg yielding. Neither of these two movements has any permanent value. Their function is mainly linguistic. They are used in stage 1 to introduce the horse to the leg aids which are used in combinations 3 and 4 (L°*, *°L). In both of these combinations, the rider applies pressure with either his right or left leg in Position 1. The other leg in Position 1 may also be used occasionally at lesser pressure, but one leg must always predominate. Such unequal pressures are what distinguishes these leg aids from those used in Combinations 1 (L°°L) and 2 (L**L). Teaching the horse preliminary obedience to the action of one leg is an important part of Stage 1. When used in a command, this leg aid tells the horse to move sideways. Once he has learned to understand these aids as commands, they then can be used in corrections. Their meaning then reverses and becomes an order not to go sideways. As commands, these leg aids tell the horse to move away from the applied pressure. As corrections, they act as a barrier, preventing the horse from moving sideways against the applied pressure. This is another application of context. If one of these aids is used before a movement, its meaning is positive; used after a movement as a correction, its movement becomes negative.

Both the pivot on the forehand and leg yielding are relatively easy exercises for the horse to learn. They have several characteristics in common. Both begin with the use of the hand aids to flex the horse's head away from the direction he will be moving. Both continue using leg aids all through the movement to tell the horse to continue sidestepping. Finally they both finish by asking the horse to return to Position Straight and go forward again. Linguistically the main difference between these two movements is one of context. The pivot on the forehand is done at a halt, leg yielding in motion at a walk. There is one other linguistic factor which may be used to distinguish between the two movements. Both require leg action to tell the horse to continue the movement, but the rider does have a choice between two different types of leg action. He can use reduplication, repeating the leg aid in a tapping action. He can also use a continuing pressure, which drops in pressure as the horse begins to respond to the original command. Personally I prefer to use reduplication to gain a step by

18. This is what Position Left and Right look like as part of an aid combination in Stage 1 or on a straight line in response to Combination 3. A finished horse, flexing to the inside as he moves around the arena, shows a more pronounced lateral flexion. To obtain this, the rider should use Combination 5.

18a. Position Left.

18b. Position Right.

step control in pivoting and a continuous pressure for sidestepping in motion, but this is a matter of choice. The rider can use one type of action for both movements or one type for the pivot and one for the leg yielding. If he uses both types of actions, this then becomes another linguistic clue, differentiating between the two movements.

To execute a pivot on the forehand, the horse must first be brought to a halt. Then, to obtain a pivot left, the rider puts the horse into Position Right and begins to apply pressure with his right leg. The horse should respond by moving his hindquarters to the left, pivoting around his inside foreleg. As his hind legs continue to step across each other, he has to describe a very small circle with his right foreleg and keep replacing his left foreleg in the same spot at a different angle. The opposite situation occurs in the pivot on the hindquarters. There the horse crosses his front legs, pivoting around his inside hind leg. As the pivot continues, he has to make the same minor adjustments with his hind legs as he did with his forelegs in the pivot on the forehand. This concentration on different ends of the horse explains the major difference in the value of these two exercises. The pivot on the hindquarters encourages the horse to carry more weight on his hindquarters, the pivot on the forehand discourages it. Therefore, the pivot on the hindquarters has permanent value, the pivot on the forehand does not. Once the horse has learned to understand this exercise linguistically, it should no longer be used.

Leg yielding has even a more limited value than the pivot on the forehand. As has already been stated, it is carried out while the horse is in motion at a walk. This exercise is always done with the horse facing the wall at an oblique angle. The more acute this angle is, the more difficult the exercise is for the horse. The wall is used to help the horse understand that he is not supposed to go forwards. To execute leg yielding to the right, the rider begins as the horse is walking around the ring on the right hand. As he comes into a corner, he heads the horse towards the wall at an angle of at least 45 degrees. He then uses his hand aids to put the horse in Position Left, flexing him away from the direction in which he is moving. As he does this, he starts applying pressure with his left leg. The horse should respond by moving sideways to the right. The aids are, of course, reversed to obtain leg yielding to the left. This exercise is, in my opinion, helpful only if the horse is using sidestepping as an evasion of going forward. Spending a little time on leg yielding can help cure this problem. However, if this difficulty does not exist, then I see no reason to use it at all. Unfortunately leg yielding is actually an incorrect version of the

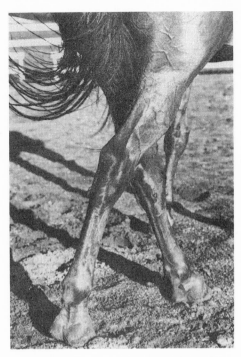

19a. A pivot on the forehand to the left. The horse is crossing his hind legs, stepping around his inside (left) foreleg, which also shows in the picture.

19b. A pivot on the hindquarters to the right. The horse is crossing his front legs, stepping around his inside (right) leg. There is noticeably more strain on this leg than there is on the left hind leg.

full pass and half pass which the horse will be taught later. In these more advanced exercises, the horse must always be flexed in the direction to which he is moving, not away from it. As I learned the hard way, too much time spent on leg yielding can create problems in getting the correct flexion in the more difficult exercises.

Combination 3 (L*°, °*L) may also play a role as a correction. Since all horses are one-sided, just as people are one-handed, most green horses do tend to carry themselves slightly to one side as they move forward. Combination 3 can be used to correct this sideways twist. This process is usually referred to in the equestrian literature as using unilateral half halts. In my opinion, there is no need to worry about this problem. It usually corrects itself as the horse is ridden forward into the bit and gymnastic exercises are used to supple him up. However, if you are concerned about it; then Podhajsky's book contains the best discussion. He explains very clearly the relationship between the horse's hollow and stiff sides and the use of unilateral half halts. Since this is not a problem which has ever concerned me, I must refer the interested reader to this discussion.

Unlike Combination 3 (L*°, °*L), Combination 4 (L°*, *°L) has a very critical role to play as a correction. In conjunction with Combination 1 (L°°L), it is used to enforce obedience to rule 1. Any time the horse tries to evade going forward by changing direction, Combination 4 is used to correct him. This is one reason why the pivot on the forehand and/or leg yielding should be used to explain its leg aids to the horse. I have seen many complicated discussions as to what the rider is supposed to do if the horse shies or runs out at a jump. They are usually too complicated for my understanding. In particular, I have never been able to figure out how the shoulder-in is supposed to be applied in such situations. In my opinion, the first thing is to make sure that you are not attempting to force the horse to do something unreasonable. Most fights between horse and rider are caused by just such demands. Given a reasonable demand, the horse still has to have some minimal understanding of the aids. This is why young horses should never be asked to do anything very complicated or difficult. However, problems can still arise even with the best trained horse. Any horse can become momentarily frightened or disobedient. In such situations, all a horse wants to do is whirl around and run way from the object of his fear or resentment. If the rider can prevent the whirl or pivot, he can also prevent the run away and eventually persuade the horse into obedience. In such circumstances, Combination 4 is very useful. If the horse wants to shy to the left,

20a. Leg yielding. Although the horse is stepping to her right, her body is curved to the left, away from the direction in which she is moving. With a green horse, the angle between the horse's body and the fence would be less acute.

20b. The full pass right. The horse is stepping in the same direction as in a., but now her body is relatively straight and she is not flexed away from the direction of the motion.

the rider should use his right hand to keep him looking at the object of which he is afraid. He should also use his left leg to tell the horse not to go sideways. These aids should be alternated with an emphatic use of Combination 1 to tell the horse to go forward. Using these two combinations together is a technique which I have used very successfully for years.

Combination 4 (L°*, *°L) is used to enforce obedience to rule 1, long before it is used to teach specific exercises. By the end of Stage 1, the horse should be reasonably willing to obey rule 1. The trainer can then proceed to use Combination 4 in Stage 2 to teach the horse three basic exercises. They are the pivot on the hindquarters, the full pass, and the half pass (two-tracking). The pivot on the hindquarters is usually taught to the horse early in Stage 2. This exercise can be done from either a halt or a walk. It is usually taught to the horse first at a halt and then practiced only in motion. The full pass begins and ends at a halt. In it, the horse steps sideways at a walk at a 90-degree angle. Its permanent value is rather limited, but it is a useful introduction to the half pass. Rather than wasting time on leg yielding, I prefer to use this exercise at a relatively early stage in training. The half pass is an extremely important gymnastic exercise. To do it well, the horse needs to be exceptionally supple and well balanced. This exercise is the movement in which the horse moves forward and sideways at a 45-degree angle. It can be done both at a walk and a trot. It is introduced rather late in Stage 2 and practiced mainly at a trot. Both the pivot on the hindquarters and the half pass can also be done at a canter, but these exercises belong in the realm of high school dressage.

The commands for all three of these exercises do have some linguistic similarities. First, they all require that the horse be flexed in the direction to which he is moving. For the purpose of practical dressage, I think it is sufficient if the horse is just looking in the right direction. However, when the pivot on the hindquarters and the half pass are executed perfectly, they do show a definite degree of lateral flexion. In my experience, the novice horse and rider have enough trouble just getting the sideways movement without the wrong flexion. Concern with perfection and lateral flexion should be left, in my opinion, for the expert and those who are interested in high school dressage. Of course, with a well-schooled horse, maintaining Position Right or Left always involves a slight degree of lateral flexion. The second similarity among the three exercises is that the leg aids must be repeated or continued to tell the horse how long the exercise should

21. *These two pictures show quite an adequate half pass for the purposes of practical dressage. The horse is moving forward and to his right. A high school specialist would be expected to take a much longer sideways step and to show better lateral flexion.*

21a. *To get the right light, we had to execute this movement out of the short side, instead of the long side of the arena. The horse therefore is passing F on his way across the arena towards E. He is correctly leading the movement with his shoulders, looking in the direction to which he is moving. He is in the process of bringing his left hind leg in front of his right one.*

21b. *The horse has now gained ground both to the side and forward, still maintaining a definite Position Right. He is now crossing his front legs.*

be carried on. Again, the rider has a choice between reduplication and a continuing pressure for the half pass. However, this choice is up to the individual. All three of these exercises also have in common the problem of position. Since they are all taught in Stage 2, the horse might well already be flexed in the correct direction. If this is true, no hand aids need to be used in the original command. However, if the exercise involves a change in direction, it usually finishes with an order telling the horse to switch to the new, correct position. If this order is necessary, it is accompanied by the one telling the horse to return to going straight forward again. In this case, the command to go straight forward would usually be given when the horse is passing through Position Straight. Of course, in the full pass both of these commands would have to be preceded by a halt.

There are also linguistic differences among the three exercises. These differences can be brought out by discussing a specific command. To execute a pivot on the hindquarters right, the rider begins with two choices. He can start the exercise from a halt or from a walk. If the horse is in motion, the command sequence must begin with a half halt. As the horse responds to this and hesitates, the order for the pivot is given. If the hand aids are necessary, they should be applied slightly before the leg aids. The horse should be in Position Right. As the horse assumes this position, the rider begins to apply his left leg. The horse should respond by pivoting to the right. In all these exercises, the left leg is used to ask the horse to move to the right. The command for the pivot right has several characteristics which distinguish it linguistically from the ones used for the full pass right or the half pass right. First, if the hand aids are necessary, they precede the leg aids. In the other two exercises, the leg aids are used first. In them, the horse is placed in position after he has started to step sideways. The second difference is in leg pressure. The leg aids for the pivot are used at a lighter level than for the full pass or half pass. This is an obvious application of rule 4. In pivoting only part of the horse moves sideways; in the other exercises, all of the horse moves sideways. Finally, the only linguistic difference between the full pass and the half pass is one of context. The full pass begins at a halt, the half pass in motion.

Obviously the horse needs time to learn to do all the exercises associated with Combinations 3 (L*○, ○*L) and 4 (L○* *○L). Since these movements are rather unnatural for the horse, he should be asked at first for only one or two steps of a pivot and to sidestep just a short distance. If the trainer attempts to force these exercises too fast, the horse is liable to rebel against what he considers to be unreasonable demands. The horse also needs time to learn to understand them linguistically. Misunderstandings are bound to occur at first. In correcting the horse with Combinations 3 and 4, it is always the leg aids that should be accentuated. If the horse fails to respond adequately, the rider should reapply his commanding leg at a higher pressure level. If the horse overresponds, the other leg comes into action to act as a barrier. Applying corrections in this fashion may involve some rather quick switching of leg aids, but they may overlap as long as they are still at unequal pressure levels. An advanced rider may, of course, also use both legs at unequal pressures to encourage lateral flexion.

The function of the exercises associated with Combinations 3 (L*○, ○*L) and 4 (L○*, *○L) can be summed up in one word—maneuverability. With the exception of the half pass, none of them is particularly valuable gymnastically. This is why less training time is spent on them, than on exercises such as circles and gait transitions. Despite the fact that these exercises are not as demanding physically, the horse still needs time to learn to do them well. The half pass, of course, is particularly difficult to execute well. However, the main function of Combinations 3 and 4 is to give the rider the ability to place his horse very precisely. In this sense, the exercises associated with them have immense practical value. Such precise control comes in very handy when working in company, dodging tree trunks in the woods, and going through gates. This increased maneuverability is also reflected in the use of Combinations 3 and 4 to enforce rule 1. Any horse is going to shy or resist going forward occasionally. The gain in control is well worth the time spent on these exercises.

14

Combination 5

Unlike all of the other combinations, Combination 5 (L°*L, L*°L) is not used to enforce any of the three basic rules. It functions only as a command for all of the exercises requiring lateral flexion. While executing any of these exercises, it is assumed that the horse is obeying all three rules. If he breaks one or more of them, then other combinations must be used to correct him. As was mentioned in chapter 5, the circle is the basic exercise for promoting lateral flexion. The horse learns to circle first, then all of the other lateral exercises are defined for him in relation to this basic command. Since all turns in dressage are defined as part of a circle, there is no fundamental difference between them. The only real distinction is that a turn usually ends sooner. Combination 5 then is used for all changes of direction which are not based on pivoting or side-stepping. Due to the problem of leads, Combination 5, instead of Combination 1 (L°°L), is also used to ask for correct canter departures. Large circles, wide turns, and canter departures are taught to the horse in Stage 1. Correctly executed, they all require a mild degree of lateral flexion. In Stage 2, cultivating lateral flexion becomes extremely important. The horse is first asked for smaller circles; then for counter cantering, the shoulder-in, and finally for the haunches-in or out. By the end of this training, all of these exercises should have helped the horse develop a high degree of lateral flexibility.

Since the circle is the basic exercise for Combination 5 (L°*L, L*°L), it obviously should be discussed first. The horse's training begins with the largest possible circle at a slow gait and ends with the smallest possible circle at a canter. The smaller the circle, the more difficult are the required flexions and balance adjustments for the horse. The faster the gait, the harder it is for the horse to correctly

22. *Flexing on a circle.*

22a. A small circle left at a canter. Horse and rider are both leaning at the same angle, illustrating the need for collection on so small a circle.

22b. A small circle right at a canter.

execute a circle of the same size. The horse begins in Stage 1 with a circle the width of the arena and ends Stage 2 with a volte. A volte is approximately 20 feet and is the smallest circle a horse can flex into. A young horse is introduced to circles almost from the time he is first mounted. A horse, who has spent enough time on a lunge line, usually discovers a large circle with relative ease. As soon as the horse has grasped the basic aids, Combination 5 can be used for wide turns. The horses can also then be introduced to the various circular exercises. There is a practically infinite number of combinations of straight lines, circles, half circles, and turns. The standard patterns are shown in Figure 6. The trainer, however, should beware of limiting his practice to the specific exercises which appear in the dressage tests. He should constantly vary the place, size, degree of turn, and the combinations he uses. Horses quickly learn to follow repeated routines and they are supposed to respond to the aids, not to memorized patterns. Of

Figure 6A

The Circular Exercises

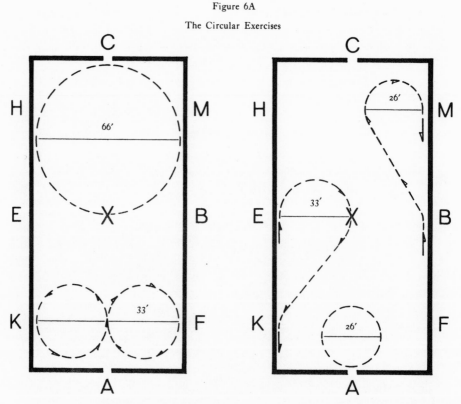

All of these can be done anywhere in the arena and at any size the horse is capable of handling.

Figure 6B

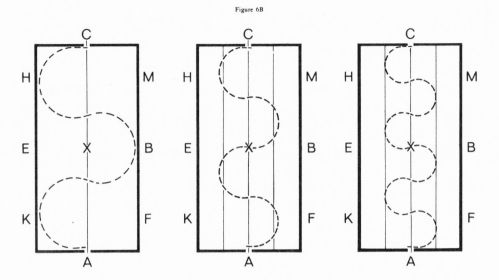

course, the need for such ingenuity applies to practicing all the gymnastic exercises, not just the circular ones.

The horse's increasing ability to flex into smaller and smaller circles depends on an increase in two other factors. One, of course is lateral flexibility. The other is engagement of the hindquarters or collection. The general size of a circle always depends on the degree to which the horse is collected when the order to circle is given. The same aids on the same horse might obtain a 66-ft. circle at a working canter and a volte at a collected trot. The smaller the circle, the more the horse must be collected beforehand. Within this general limitation, the rider's aids determine the exact size and length of the circle. To obtain a circle right, the rider would use C5B (L°*L). He first asks the horse for Position Right. Of course, in Stage 2 the horse might well already be in the correct position. As the horse begins to change his head position, the rider drops his outside or left leg back into Position 2 and begins to apply his legs. It is the amount of the position change and the strength of the leg aids which determine the precise size of the circle. The more pronounced the position and the stronger the leg aids, the smaller should be the circle. When the horse receives the original command to circle, he should begin to flex to the right, moving off a straight line and onto a circular path. A trained horse continues on this path until his rider gives him permission to go straight again or asks him to flex in the other direction. Of course, an experienced horse may anticipate a new order at the 90°, 180°, or

360° point, but he still waits for permission to change direction or flexion.

The above discussion only describes what is supposed to happen with a well-trained horse. Obviously achieving a correct circle with a green horse is not quite so simple. If the horse fails to respond properly, corrections for Combination 5 (L°*L, L*°L) can be made with both the hand and leg aids. In using the hand aids for major corrections, Combination 5 is different from all the other aid combinations. In them, only the leg aids are accentuated to correct the horse. As was stated in chapter 12, in combinations 1 (L°°L) and 2 (L**L) corrections were made by equally increasing the pressure levels of both legs in Position 1. Normally the rider uses only one leg at a time for both commands and corrections in combinations 3 (L*°, °*L) and 4 (L°*, *°L). Since in these combinations the rider has his legs in Position 1, if he uses both legs together, he is liable to confuse the horse. Any time the rider applies equal pressures with both legs, he is asking the horse for more engagement of the hindquarters. This is true even if the rider has one leg in Position 2. If the rider applies equal pressures with both of the leg aids for Combination 5, they take on a double meaning. They then ask the horse for more impulsion, as well as for more lateral flexion. When Combination 5 is used for corrections, if the rider simply accentuates both legs at unequal pressures, then he is just asking for more lateral flexion. In this case, the raise in pressure is usually more pronounced with the outside leg.

So far in discussing the corrective leg aids for all the combinations, the assumption has been made that the horse was correctly flexed in Position Straight, Right, or Left. If he was not, the appropriate hand aids (*° °*) should be used to correct him. This is not often necessary since maintaining correct position rarely represents much of a problem with a horse. However, there is one difficulty which frequently occurs when Combination 5 (L°*L, L*°L) is used to ask a stiff horse for lateral flexion. Since the horse finds it much easier to bend his neck than his body, he frequently tries to evade the correct flexion by overbending his neck. To cure this evasion, the rider should try to prevent the overflexion by fixing his outside hand. If the horse overbends to the right, he fixes his left hand. If he overbends to the left, he fixes his right hand. Essentially what the rider does is reverse half of his normal hand aids. He tenses the opposite hand, but without giving with the other. If he gave as he normally does, the horse would probably switch to the opposite head position, instead of just stopping the overflexion. Neither of these corrective hand aids should be used without the appropriate leg aids. To correct overbending right, the aid combination used would be *LL. To correct overbending left, they would be LL*. This is the one situation in which the rider's hand aids do not need to be applied at equal pressures.

There seems to be some difference of opinion regarding the use of the outside leg in Combination 5 (L°*L, L*°L). Personally, I apply pressure with this leg mainly as a corrective. Simply dropping the leg back into Position 2 is, in my opinion, significant enough in itself to serve as an aid with a schooled horse. However, some people do believe in applying pressure with this leg in a command. As long as both leg aids remain at unequal pressure levels, this does not represent a problem. I feel that using no pressure with the outside leg in a command, makes its application as a corrective more emphatic, but this is a personal preference. In all of the exercises associated with Combination 5, the outside leg remains back in Position 2 until the exercise is completed. Even if no pressure is applied, this means that a leg aid is continued throughout the exercise. To maintain the correct flexion, no more may be necessary with a trained horse. However, with a young one, the leg aids may have to be repeated at almost every step to prevent him from losing the lateral flexion.

Enough has now been said about the basic aids in Combination 5 (L°*L, L*°L). Since a turn represents part of a circle, this combination is probably the most used combination of all. Due to the rectangular shape of the dressage arena, the horse has to cope with four turns every time he goes once around. A schooled horse executes this as four straight lines and four quarter voltes. A young horse goes straight down the long sides and around the short sides as though they were half circles. A horse should never be asked to turn through a corner on an arc which is any smaller than the circle he can do in the open. As the horse develops his ability to execute smaller and smaller circles, he can be asked to turn sharper and sharper corners. By the time the horse is ready to work out his corners as quarter voltes, he is also ready to learn to maintain Position Right or Left. A horse was introduced to these positions by using Combination 3 (L*°, °*L) on a straight line. To teach him to stay in position, Combination 5 should be used. This allows the rider to ask him for a continuous flexion to the inside, which simply becomes more pronounced through the corners. Eventually maintaining position becomes almost automatic with a horse, so that the lighest touch with the inside leg is enough to tell him when to turn through the corner. Indeed, to indicate a turn with a really responsive horse, all the rider really has to do is look where he wants to go.

Now that turns and circles have been discussed, the next use of Combination 5 (L°*L, L*°L) is for canter departures. Since the rider needs to be able to specify a lead, he cannot use Combination 1 (L°°L for this gait change. A horse at a canter usually maintains a slight flexion towards his leading side. Since a horse is stiffer on one side, he will tend to prefer one lead. A horse always learns a new exercise more easily on his good side. This is especially true of leads. Some horses may be initially so stiff to one side, that it is almost impossible to get them to canter on that lead. This is one of the reasons why correct canter departures are usually taught after the horse has learned to flex on a large circle at a trot. These circles help loosen up his bad side. A large circle is also the best place to ask the young horse for a canter. There are two reasons for this. First, the horse is already correctly flexed to the inside, so all the rider has to do is apply his leg aids and give with both hands. Second, if the horse is already on a circle, he is less liable to confuse the circle and canter commands. In any case, for a canter departure, the horse first must be put in the correct position, then the rider applies his leg aids and gives with both hands. He must add these hand aids (°°) to Combination 5, so the horse understands that he is supposed to canter, not circle.

There is no subject more controversial in horsemanship than how to get the correct lead at a canter. This conflict is a perfect illustration of the arbitrary nature of communication between horse and rider. Any aids will do, so long as both parties know what they are supposed to be. The advantage of the ones used in dressage is that they can be used later to define new commands. Now, the horse first learns to canter from a trot. He is then introduced to cantering from a walk and halt in Stage 1. Once he has learned to back, he can also be asked to canter on after that exercise. There is a step in both the trot and walk at which the horse can switch directly into a canter. He should be expected to canter directly from a walk fairly soon. He can also go directly from a halt into a canter, but this is a gymnastic feat which cannot be expected of him until late in Stage 2. Even if the horse seems to be going directly into a canter, he is probably taking one or two preparatory steps and actually switiching from a walk. Like any gait changes, the more extreme the change, the stronger should the leg aids be. As the horse learns to canter from each point or gait level, he can also be asked to change leads through it. To

23. *The horse should first be asked to counter canter on the outside lead down the long side of the arena. This series(a.–c.) shows a simple change of lead in the corner. The change in the horse's head position—from right to straight to left—is particularly noticeable.*

23a. *Coming around the corner on the right lead with the horse beautifully flexed to the inside.*

23b. *A few steps at a walk in Position Straight.*

23c. Transition into the left lead with the horse flexed to the outside.

23d. The true counter canter. The horse is circling to the right on the left lead. The gymnastics required by this exercise show up clearly in this picture. The horse is well flexed, yet taking an extra long step to balance herself. Aside from the gymnastic effect, it can be very useful to have a horse who is well balanced on the outside lead.

obtain a change, the rider simply uses Combination 2 (L**L) to bring the horse down to the desired point and then asks him to canter on again on the opposite lead.

In theory, a change of leads is quite simple. In practice, it presents some serious complications. The difficulty is mainly a question of anticipation. The horse soon learns to expect a lead change with a direction change at a canter. He then tends to resist breaking gait and will often excitedly plunge back into a canter without changing his lead. This problem is particularly acute in changing through a walk. The cure seems to be variety. The trainer should constantly vary the place of change, its gait level, and the time spent at the intervening gait. He can also alternate between changing leads and not returning to a canter. Endless practice is usually required before these transitions become consistently smooth and effortless. Once the horse has mastered lead changes, he can be introduced to counter cantering. The easiest way to do this is to ask him to counter canter down the long side of the arena. This, of course, requires a simple change of lead in both corners, one into the counter canter and one out of it. The next step is to start making very wide turns without a lead change well away from the walls of the arena. As the horse improves, he can be asked to make narrower turns and eventually to counter canter through the corners of the arena. In my experience, the key both to picking up and maintaining the counter canter seems to be keeping the horse's head sufficiently flexed to the outside. If the rider does this, a horse who has been taught correct canter departures should have very little trouble understanding this exercise. It has then been defined for him in the context of what he already knows.

There are three more exercises associated with Combination 5 (L°*L, L*°L). They are the shoulder-in, the haunches-in, and the haunches-out. In all of these exercises the horse moves on two tracks, just as he does in the half pass. The difference is that in the half pass he goes forwards and sideways, in the shoulder-in and haunches-in or out he continues going forwards while flexing part of his body off of a straight line. As Fig. 5 shows, all of these exercises involve lateral flexion. If the top half of the horse doing the shoulder-in were put together with the bottom half of the horse doing the haunches-in, they would form a perfect flexion for a circle. The shoulder-in accentuates the front part of this flexion, the haunches-in the back part. There is no real difference gymnastically or linguistically between the shoulder-in or out or the haunches-in or out. The distinction between them is merely based on the relationship of the horse's body to the wall of the arena. It is perfectly possible to do a shoulder-out, even though this exercise is not normally practiced and the haunches-out is. All of these exercises are best taught to the horse in relation to the circle. For a shoulder-in the rider accentuates his inside leg, for a haunches-in he accentuates his outside leg. This is another obvious application of rule 4. In all of the other exercises associated with Combination 5, the rider first puts the horse into position with his hand aids, and then uses his leg aids. For the shoulder-in and the haunches-in or out, the opposite is true. The rider first obtains the lateral flexion with his leg aids, and then allows the horse to assume the correct position with his hands. I have come to the conclusion that not one of these three exercises has any value in practical dressage. There seems to be no gymnastic or linguistic benefit to be gained from them that cannot be obtained just as well through the regular circular exercises. Considering the importance of teaching the horse to go straight, I also object to deliberately teaching the horse to twist his body off of a straight line. The critical importance of lateral flexibility cannot be questioned, but I just am not convinced that these exercises are either a safe or good means of developing it.

Now that all the exercises, aid combinations, and corrections have

Figure 7
Lateral Flexion on Two Tracks

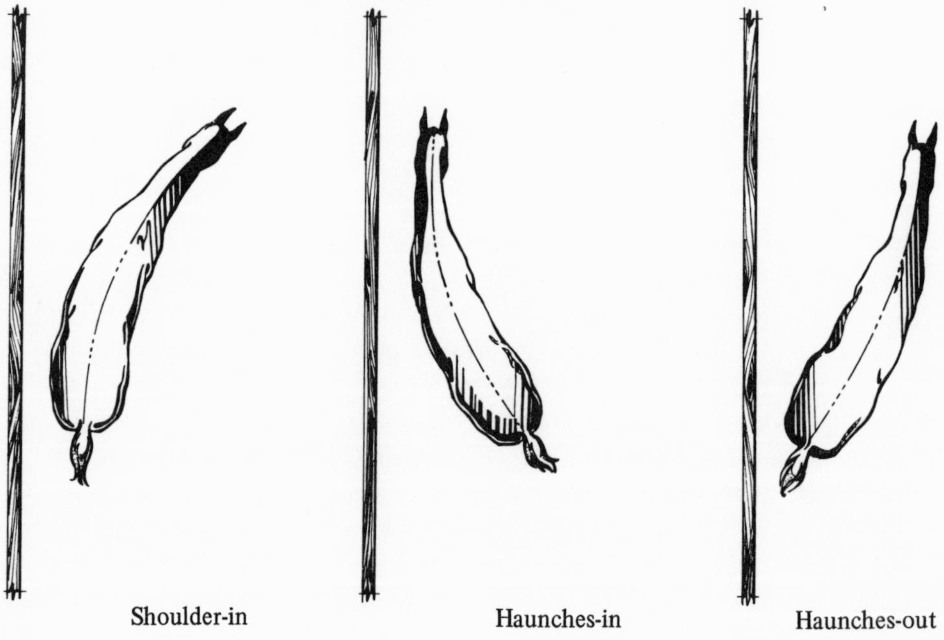

Shoulder-in   Haunches-in   Haunches-out

been discussed, the full complexity of the dressage communication system should be apparent. Mastering it requires a great deal of time and effort for horse and rider alike. As the horse gradually acquires linguistic competence, he learns to anticipate which aid combinations will be used for what class of orders in what circumstances. He also eventually comes to understand the general meaning of each set of hand or leg aids. (See Table IV) The preceding pages should by now have well defined all of these semantic relationships. Just as a horse must learn to understand them, so must the rider. An experienced rider must be able to flexibly apply his knowledge, building whatever command sequences are appropriate to the specific situation. Without stopping for thought, he must be able to apply the right aid combination, in the right order, at the right pressure levels, and with the right amount of reduplication. Any time he has to stop and think about what aids to use, they are usually too late to be very effective. The horse too should not have to stop for thought. Like the rider, he should be able to react on the basis of physical habits and unconscious understanding. Acquiring this level of competence obviously requires endless hours of practice for both. There is always plenty of room for error in this process, which is why the language of the aids always utilizes multiple clues to establish meaning. Just the same, mistakes and their corrections are the inevitable accompaniment to any training program.

Table IV, General Meanings for Sets of Aids

1. Both hands relax to an equal degree (^{OO})—Go forward.
2. Both hands tense to an equal degree (**)—Collect.
3. Left hand tenses, right hand relaxes to an equal degree (*^{O})—Position Left
4. Right hand tenses, left hand relaxes to an equal degree (^{O}*)—Position Right
5. Both legs applied actively in Position 1 (LL)—More engagement of the hindquarters
6. One leg applied in Position 1, the other left passive or applied at a markedly lesser degree of pressure (L L)—Go sideways (as a command preceding action by the horse) or Don't go sideways (as a correction following action by the horse)
7. One leg applied in Position 1, the other left passive or applied in Position 2 (LL LL)—Lateral flexion.
    While the hand aids must never be used alone, a trained horse will understand simple orders when they are conveyed only by the leg aids. This is a very useful ability since it allows the rider to control the horse when he is off contact. Of course, without the hand aids, the rider does lose a great deal of precision and quickness of response.

Source Materials and Suggested Readings

Rather obviously the linguistic, rather than the gymnastic, aspects of the basic exercises has been emphasized in Part 4. This is because they have been the least adequately handled in the literature. Other than brief definitions, I have avoided discussing their physical aspects. I think that Wynmalen's *Dressage* contains some of the best basic explanations, but helpful information on the exercises can be found in almost every textbook on equitation. Beudant's book has some especially refreshing comments on the value of various exercises, as well as on overmechanistic explanations of the aids.

PART V

Horse Management
the Easy Way

15
The Equine View of Life

Regardless of how well a trainer understands the objectives of dressage and the theory of the aids, his eventual success will depend on his ability to think like a horse. A horse always has a perfectly good reason for anything he does. When he is indulging in undesirable behavior, the trainer's job is to discover what is his reason. Once the cause is discovered and dealt with, the undesirable behavior will disappear. Few riders are willing to take the time and patience to do this. The common tendency is to underrate a horse's natural abilities and to overlook how unreasonable our demands usually look to him. For example, many riders are afraid to trust the horse's agility and common sense in covering rough ground. The same people fail to ask themselves why any sane horse should jump over an obstacle he could just as well go around.

In designing a training program, the knowledgeable trainer is forced to consider the basic motivational drives which are at the bottom of much seemingly inexplicable equine behavior. Possibly the strongest and most compelling emotion a horse knows is a fear of being eaten. It is difficult for a carnivorous animal like ourselves to appreciate how this fear pervades the life of any herbivorous animal like a horse. By human standards any normal horse is an arrant coward. The guiding motto of his life is "When in doubt, run." A horse sees himself as meat on the hoof, a delicious meal for any lucky predator. His world seethes with hungry monsters whose one aim in life is having him for dinner. These fears have been bred into him through millions of years of evolution. In the wilds any horse, without sense enough to run at the slightest hint of danger, would have a remarkably short life expectancy. No rider can afford to forget that horses are very easily frightened. A terrified horse has only one desire, to flee as fast as possible from whatever has upset him. Anything or anyone in the way is liable to get trampled in the rush.

One of a horse's favorite methods of avoiding fear is staying in familiar territory. A wild herd roams through a definite area, well supplied with bolt holes and escape routes. If chased, they will simply travel in a large circle, always returning to home base. A domesticated horse is just as reluctant to leave his familiar pasture or stable. One of the signs of a well-trained horse is that he travels just as fast away from home as he does towards it. Moyra Williams (1957) discovered that horses seem to possess a homing instinct almost like that of pigeons. Carried off into strange country and without any sensory clues to help, her horses knew which direction to go to get home. Using a trial-and-error process, often backtracking around obstacles such as fenced-in fields, they eventually made it home.

A horse's attachment to familiar territory is partially due to his need for security. What frightens a horse the most is the half familiar. In completely strange surroundings, he doesn't know of what to be frightened. In familiar surroundings, he will not be afraid until something strange is introduced. In the wild the slightest alteration from normal can mean that a predator is lurking. No horse in his right mind ever stays around long enough to discover if his initial suspicions were correct. Domesticated horses are just as afraid of the half familiar. I have seen a whole herd thrown into a panic just because the position of their pasture gate had been altered. Carrying a gun or wearing a pair of skis can change a friendly human into a fire-breathing dragon.

The horse's other major defense against fear is surrounding himself with plenty of equine company. No horse ever wants to stay alone. Any company is better than none. A newcomer, however much he is chivied and chased, will never leave the vicinity of the herd he wants so desperately to join. Belonging to a herd has several advantages in the wild. Its individual members can pool their knowledge of the country and predator hunting techniques. Sentry duty can also be shared. In any herd, wild or domestic, all of the horses will never lie down at once. One or two always remain on their feet as guards. Moyra Williams (1957) found that this held true even at night in the stable. When domestic horses go out together on a trail ride, the lead horse is always more alert. It is his job to watch for danger.

A horse herd, however, is not an amorphous mass nor is it a democratic society. Social relationships within the herd are governed by a hierarchical arrangement. Status is determined by who can kick

24a. Togetherness is an equine thing.

24b. No horse really enjoys working alone.

or bite whom without retaliation. Settling a newcomer's position in this hierarchy always involves a number of trial fights to establish who he can dominate. The struggle for power in a modern corporation is much like the same struggle within a horse herd. Only the status symbols are different. Instead of the biggest office, the top horse gets in the barn first at feeding time. Each young horse has to learn a new set of manners under saddle. He must learn to ignore all of the status relationships which govern so much of his behavior in a herd. He soon discovers that the other horses will not bite or kick him and that he will not be allowed to attack them. A well-trained horse works quietly behind, in front of, or beside other horses. He also ignores the presence of either his equine friends or enemies. Drill work is an excellent method of establishing these new patterns of behavior, as are the special exercises for hunters described by Littauer (1956).

In addition to a new set of company manners, a young horse must learn to overcome many of his instinctive drives. He must patiently be taught to leave his safe, familiar home and his equine friends. Both of these demands seem outrageously unreasonable to a horse at first. Eventually he discovers that the outside world is really not as dangerous as it looks and that he is not alone as long as he has a rider with him. To help his equine pupil learn these new attitudes, an intelligent trainer tries to anticipate circumstances that might frighten or upset him. He then gradually exposes his pupil to increasingly upsetting situations. Each time the horse overcomes his fears, it is that much easier to reassure him the next time. On their first trips into the unknown, the company of a calm, well-behaved, older horse can be very helpful. Such an equine schoolmaster gives a colt a model of good behavior to imitate. This horse can show him that various objects aren't really as frightening as they look and that it is possible to go through such hazards as mud or water. Bad footing almost always terrifies a horse because he is afraid of being trapped and unable to run. Once a colt goes well in company, he then can be taken out alone over familiar trails. Eventually, of course, he should willingly go anywhere, alone or with other horses.

Establishing these new attitudes and patterns of behavior should be an essential part of any horse's training. Unfortunately it is rarely done thoroughly enough. This explains why most so-called pleasure horses have acquired so many unpleasant vices. Just getting a colt to accept calmly the presence of a rider on his back is not enough. He has to be re-educated. Just as a young child has to learn how to behave

25. *A coward reformed. Gay is calmly negotiating a wide ditch. Three years ago she would have refused to have anything to do with such an obvious equine trap.*

to be an accepted member of a human society, a young horse has to learn that carrying a rider involves many radical changes in his normal behavior patterns. Unless he is patiently and carefully helped to learn these alterations, he is liable to indulge in all kinds of unacceptable behavior. Much of the initial training of a young horse involves explaining to him what he is not supposed to do. Under saddle he should not kick, bite, buck, rear, or run away. He must not be afraid to leave home or to work alone. Finally, he has to learn not to pay attention to any other horses, but to concentrate on following his rider's orders.

Fortunately horses and humans can relate to each other with relative ease. Part of the reason for this lies in our biological heritage. On the evolutionary scale, horses as mammals are our close cousins. They share many of our basic emotions and motivations. They know the same need for security, membership in a social group, and status. They feel fear, pain, anger, hatred, and affection for other horses. Their basic personalities can be just as variable as those of people. A horse can be aggressive or nonaggressive, dignified or happy-go-lucky, vain or unassuming, timid and nervous, or calm and sensible.

However, these similarities do not mean that a horse sees the world from the same viewpoint as we do. Any human who saw a sabre-toothed tiger behind every bush would be quite insane. This is perfectly normal behavior for a horse. Humans can enjoy being alone; any horse regards this as torture by solitary confinement.

This brings us to the much disputed matter of equine intelligence. Even scientists, who ought to know better, still persist in making comparisons of intelligence between species. It is legitimate to say that one horse is more intelligent than another, but there is very little point in comparing horses to humans. A horse has no reason to solve mathematical puzzles, but he can size up a rider faster than any riding instructor can. No animal should be asked to solve a problem that is not relevant to him. In my experience a horse can be extremely stupid when it pays him to be stupid and extremely smart when it pays him to be smart. Moyra Williams (1957) discovered that horses look so dumb in the usual laboratory experiments because they refuse to regard food as a reward. The idea of exerting effort to gain food is utterly alien to the equine mentality. A horse may spend most of his waking life eating, but his energy is directed towards avoiding being eaten in the wild and avoiding work in domestic life. Since a horse never exerts any effort to gain food, even giving him special treats will not motivate him to do anything.

If horses are not born stupid, the way in which we treat them often makes them so. Keeping a horse locked up in a small pasture or in a stall does little to develop his intelligence. A wild horse has to work at staying alive. He also roams through relatively large areas, encountering many surprises, puzzles, and problems as he does so. Learning to conduct himself properly in a herd also develops a horse's mentality, as does correct training. A horse needs to be free of the barn at least part of the time. He also needs the emotional security of being a recognized member of herd society. I have seen many a horse's disposition soured from being kept in all the time. Although I may ride them twice as much, I find I actually accomplish less training when my horses can't be turned out. Getting them to relax and move freely forward is so much more difficult.

I have never understood why a horse must necessarily be considered inferior just because he is different. A horse's viewpoint may not be ours, but this does not make him unintelligent. Indeed, when it comes to memory, he can outclass most people. I doubt if any human could travel fast across rough country and remember it the way a horse can. Far too often horses are punished and called stupid for

26. *The equine idea of heaven.*

26a. *Horses need to be free in the pasture with their friends. Gay is in the foreground.*

26b. *The easy way to finish cooling out on a hot day.*

what is perfectly natural behavior to them. At the same time they are expected to easily grasp and carry out orders which make very little sense to them. Few riders ever stop and consider how complicated, from a horse's point of view, are many of the things we ask them to do. No horse really sees any point to going round and round a ring, especially when he has to exert the energy demanded by jumping or dressage. Chasing after a polo ball, a fox, or a cow looks even more ridiculous to a horse. Once he has learned one of these social games, a horse may come to enjoy them; but first he does have to be patiently taught how to play them. We may claim horses are stupid; I suspect they think we are quite mad.

16
Management Styles

The way in which a trainer perceives equine nature will have a pro-
found effect on the results he will get from the horse. A rider's view
of the horse's potential talents influences both how he handles the
horse and what he expects to get back from him. Any opinion or definition of equine nature tends to re-inforce itself because the horse
senses it and conducts himself accordingly. If you expect a horse to
be stupid, he will exhibit little sign of intelligence. If you assume a
horse has some brains and common sense, he will show them. A
trainer's expectations can greatly influence an animal. For example,
it is a matter of scientific fact that rats will run mazes faster if their
trainers are told that their rats are exceptionally intelligent. There
are four common views of equine nature, each one of which leads to a
different management style. These distinctive styles tend to produce
noticeably different results, from well-behaved horses to ruined or
rebellious slaves.

Two of these identifiable viewpoints are relatively useless for
serious training, although they are frequently found among riders.
First, there are certain callous people who regard horses as though
they were machines. Their horses are never supposed to suffer from
exhaustion, hunger, or thirst. This is reprehensible enough among
back-yard horse owners or at those stables which rent out horses by
the hour. Unfortunately this attitude also creeps into show circles
among people who cannot plead ignorance as an excuse. Many riders
don't seem to care about damaging the horse, as long as they can
win. This exploitive approach is responsible for the use of drugs
and ruins horses right and left. There are some riders who go through
two or three horses in a show season. If the horse doesn't break down
physically under this type of abuse, he becomes excessively nervous or

turns sullen. In any case, he can no longer be safely ridden. This approach is obviously futile for serious training. No horse, who is in pain, half-starved, doped, or frightened out of what wits he does possess, is capable of learning anything.

The opposite of this tyrannical approach is the sentimental one exhibited by so many children or amateurs. This viewpoint is usually based on the romantic and misleading image of horses that is found in the popular literature. Horses, as they are depicted in books, bear little or no resemblance to real horses. Contrary to all the story books, if a horse saves your life, it is only accidentally in the course of saving his own. Another persistent legend is the horse who only allows one person to ride him. A horse may go better for someone he knows and trusts, but I have yet to see a true one-man horse. This romantic viewpoint usually results in spoiling a horse rotten. A spoiled horse is just as much of a nuisance as a spoiled child and much more dangerous. No horse ever sees any reason why he should have to work for a living. From his viewpoint, he will only obey those riders who have won his respect. When it comes to inventing devious plots for avoiding work, horses have few equals. I have seen horses, by a series of clever stratagems, reduce many riders to tears or impotent anger. Many people like to think that they love their horses, but this will not motivate the horse to do anything in return. Horses may develop strong affections for other horses, but whether or not they can develop any emotional attachment to humans is definitely a questionable matter. True love tries to see horses as they really are, not as we would like them to be.

The third approach to horse management is best described as authoritarian. A tyrannical rider has no interest in the feelings of his horse. An authoritarian merely assumes that horses are both stupid and naturally docile. He sees them as born slaves, whose every step must be rigidly guided and controlled for their own good. Without being cruel or unnecessarily punitive, an authoritarian trainer demands absolute submission and obedience from his horse. His role is to give the orders, the horse's is just to do as he is told. This method, supported by the linguistic and gymnastic techniques of dressage, can get good results in expert hands. However, it does have several limitations. First, it results in a horse who will only do as much as his rider is capable of making him do. Such a horse will snatch at any chance to disobey a less-skilled rider. Second, it tends to destroy a horse's natural initiative and independence. A horse, who has been taught such complete obedience, would be quite dangerous to ride through rough country. Instead of taking care of himself and watching his footing, he will depend on his rider for orders. Third, this method also destroys a horse's individuality, reducing him to the role of a soulless automaton. Such a horse may do well in competition, but he is not much fun to ride. He does not normally enjoy his work and he makes no attempt to figure out new ways to please his rider.

The fourth and final approach to training is based on a participative method of management. Anyone who uses it, as I do, sees his horse as an equal, but junior partner. He regards riding as a mutually enjoyable game, demanding different skills from each participant. His role is that of a teacher or guide, not a boss. A trainer's job is to explain the rules of the game to the horse, who should be left as free as possible to exercise his own initiative and talents in following them. A participative rider assumes that horses, although unlike humans in many respects, are far from stupid. Rather than dominating the horse, he tries to encourage him to develop his own abilities and to discover that work really can be fun. Putting this method into practice is much more difficult than it sounds. It must be based on the development of mutual trust and confidence. Establishing such a relationship demands a great deal of tact and patience on the part of the trainer. However, anyone who is willing to invest the necessary time and effort will find it more than worth-while. This method creates a horse who can be trusted to go well under any circumstances and who will exert every effort in his desire to please.

One of the difficulties in explaining participative management is that it cannot really be successfully applied until the horse has learned to behave properly under saddle. Much of the initial training of a young horse is negative in nature. Until new habits of behavior have been firmly established, a trainer can only be authoritative in his approach. The whole objective of this preliminary training is to convince the horse that the easiest way to achieve his goal of an easy life is to obey his rider. A colt has to discover that he must do as his rider asks, but that if he does so nothing is going to hurt him. A horse must respect his rider before he can learn to trust and obey him willingly. The many things a young horse must learn have already been discussed in detail in Chapters 4, 10, and 15. He has to learn to accept a saddle, bridle, and rider without fuss. He must learn to go straight forward at a particular pace until he is given permission to change. He has to learn to leave home and to work alone. He must also acquire a new set of company manners. It usually takes at least a year for a colt to acquire the attitudes which are essential to correct behavior under a rider. Straightening out a spoiled horse, who was not taught to behave properly at the beginning of his association with humans, is really a horrible job. However, if horses couldn't be taught to behave well, no beginner would ever learn to ride.

At this preliminary stage in training, both authoritarian and participative management aim at teaching the horse to respect his rider and at establishing the habit of obedience. Since the authoritarian approach is most interested in obedience, it can initially obtain better and faster results. However, once the horse is past this point, its results will be limited by what the trainer can make the horse do. On the other hand, the participative approach, although it is more time consuming in the beginning, does usually lead to better results in the long run. A participative trainer, as opposed to an authoritarian one, is more patient and persuasive in his initial approach. To him, obtaining the horse's confidence is just as important as obtaining his obedience. A horse, trained by this approach, eventually becomes utterly reliable and can be trusted in a sense that another, trained by a more authoritarian approach, never can be. As such a horse comes to trust his trainer and enjoy his work, he finally reaches a point where he really wants to please. Then he starts to use all of his innate abilities for his rider, instead of against him. He suddenly starts to make rapid progress, eventually bypassing the horse who is only doing as he is told.

As has already been mentioned, there are three psychological characteristics which are essential characteristics of the well-trained horse. They are relaxation, willingness, and attentiveness. Each of the management styles, that have been described, affect these qualities differently. The tyrannical approach never even achieves relaxation, which is a primary prerequisite for dressage training. The horse may be attentive and momentarily obedient, but this is based on fear. Such rule by terror quickly drives him into a physical or emotional breakdown. The sentimental approach does create a relaxed horse, but one who is inattentive and maliciously disobedient out of disrespect. The authoritarian method does establish an adequate degree of relaxation, obedience, and attentiveness. However, this approach will never attain the willing obedience and acute attentiveness that the participative one will. A horse who enjoys his work and wants to please offers a cheerful and generous obedience that another, who merely follows orders, will never attain. This willingness also expresses itself by paying close attention to the rider's subtlest wishes. An authoritarian rider may often call the horse to attention with Combination 2 (L**L) or by forcing him to do an artificial exercise,

27. Who trains whom? Showing appreciation for your horse's efforts is always worthwhile.

27a. Chief sweeping up a sugar lump.

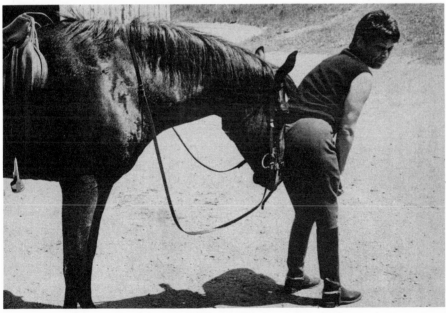

27b. Gay scratching her itching head on Cele.

such as the shoulder-in. A participative trainer has little need for such remedies, his horse should already be alert. However, this extra attentiveness is bought at the price of exercising considerable ingenuity to prevent the horse from becoming bored. Dressage work, especially if it is overdone, can be extremely dull for a horse. Keeping your training program as varied and interesting as possible is essential if you want your horse to enjoy and take pride in his work. Frequent relaxing trail rides are an excellent method of giving the horse a break from the close concentration demanded by dressage.

I do personally use and advocate the participative approach for the average amateur. The authoritarian one demands more riding skill and experience than he usually possesses. The professional is often forced into authoritarian management because of his need for quick results. The amateur, who presumably is schooling his horse to please himself, can afford to take the time and patience for the participative approach. People who ride for pleasure usually prefer a horse who has been trained by this method. Such horses may not be as successful in the show arena, but they are tremendous fun to ride. I find that my own pleasure is doubled when my horse enjoys working for me as much as I enjoy riding him. The ultimate objective of training for me is convincing the horse that he wants to do whatever I want him to do. It takes a good deal of time, patience, and tact to achieve this goal, but the results are well worth it. Then all you have to do is sit back and enjoy the results of your labors.

17
An Artistic Endeavor

Earlier parts of this book have discussed the gymnastic and communicative techniques of dressage. These aspects of training can be analyzed, categorized, and taught. The psychological side of horse handling can be learned only through experience. It cannot be taught by books, or other humans; it must be learned from the horse. Sympathy for the equine point of view is an essential part of training. Out of the many people who ride, few are real horsemen. It is an unusual rider who truly cares for his horse's opinions and who strives to establish an equal partnership with him. The ultimate objective of dressage is to fuse horse and rider into one. Together they become something more than either could separately. This unity, this relief from the inescapable loneliness of life, is the point at which dressage becomes an art. Many pundits of the dressage arena never achieve this. Most horses are limited physically as to what they can attain in dressage, but almost any horse can reach this fusion with the right rider. Regardless of what brilliant airs you and your horse can or cannot produce, if you have this wonderful sense of fusion, you have discovered what dressage is all about. At this point you start to feel your horse's emotions as though they were your own and he starts to reflect every change in your moods with his body.

One of the most remarkable things about horses is that they treat each rider exactly as he deserves. They respond to the tyrannical trainer with terrorized obedience, to the sentimental one with gleeful disobedience, to the authoritarian one with unthinking submissiveness, and to the participative one with joyous service. In my opinion, only the participative approach can succeed in achieving true fusion. There is all the difference in the world between the dull compliance of an authoritatively-trained horse and the eager willingness of one trained by the participative method. Any one can get simple obedience from a horse; it takes an artist to get a horse to the point where he enthusiastically places at your service every bit of knowledge and every ounce of skill he possesses. So often our view of equine nature limits the results we get from our training programs. A professional cannot afford to get emotionally involved with the horses he trains; this is half the fun for an amateur. It is the emotional rapport between horse and rider that turns dressage into an art; otherwise it is a mere spectacle of flashy gaits and movements. Horses in some ways size us up more realistically than we do them. Unhampered by the distorting lens of education, they judge each rider as a unique individual. As each new person approaches him, a horse thinks "Human, can you make me obey you, trust you, find pleasure in serving you?" How you treat him determines his answer to this question.

Associating with horses is always a two-way process. If you want a horse to give you his best efforts, you must first fulfill a number of his expectations. Stable management is outside of the scope of this book, but any horse must be healthy and happy before he can be interested in working very hard. Most people are so concerned with their horses' physical health, that they overlook their emotional health. Horses do need frequent opportunities to run free and to associate with other horses. The whole horse comes to a training session; a contented horse makes a much better pupil. How a training session is handled also influences a horse's response. No horse who finds working painful, uncomfortable, or exhausting is going to be very cooperative. Your training program should also be kept as interesting and varied as possible. Doing the same dull thing over and over again doesn't give a horse any incentive to please. Horses do appreciate sympathetic handling, even preferring it to good riding. They are usually quite willing to overlook your mistakes, to the extent that you are willing to overlook theirs. As long as you are reasonable in your demands, they will be reasonable in theirs. Generally speaking, the better you treat them, the better they will treat you. As long as you don't expect perfection, they won't either.

Horses, like humans, want to be treated as unique individuals. One of the major problems in handling horses is that they don't read the books that explain how they are supposed to behave. No two horses are alike and each one has to be handled differently. Some horses respond best to firm orders, others to polite requests. Some like verbal praise and encouragement, others ignore it. Analyzing your equine pupil's particular temperament and discovering the key

28. *Variety is the spice of life.*

28a. Hill climbing is an excellent gymnastic exercise.

28b. Jumping an occasional log is all part of the day's work for a good trail horse. Trotting quietly towards the log, Chief is obviously considering whether to jump it or just step over it.

28c. Over the jump, with the horse still calmly chewing his grass. We had stopped for a rest just before these pictures were taken and Chief was not about to abandon his snack.

28d. There is nothing like a good run after a lot of collected work in the ring.

to his character is one of the first steps in training. For example, I found with one of my horses that agreeing to spend equal time on cross-country work was essential to gaining his cooperation in the ring. Unfortunately few riders listen to their horses. How the horse acts before, during, and after a workout can tell you a great deal about what he thinks of you and your training program. Many horses eventually give up trying to communicate and slide into a stupor of unthinking obedience. If you want your horse to listen to you, you ought to try listening to him.

Perhaps the most difficult aspect of training for the novice is developing equestrian tact. Few riders know when and when not to insist on absolute obedience from the horse. When to be easy and when to be firm; these are the hardest decisions in training and the keys to success. One of the main problems that a nonprofessional usually encounters with the authoritarian approach is that it creates more resistance than he is able to handle. It is always better to ask for too little, than to demand so much that the horse is provoked into resentment and noncooperation. Once a horse has learned to respect his trainer, true disobedience is actually quite rare. He will then make mistakes out of fear, misunderstanding, or a physical inability to respond. Horses do not have to be forced to obey every order. If you have made a mistake and asked too much, the best policy is usually to withdraw the order before the misunderstanding escalates into a major conflict. Before starting an argument, it is always well to make sure that your original request and expectations were reasonable; otherwise, you may be asking for serious trouble.

Most riders tend to underrate their horse's intelligence and overrate their docility. Horses always do as they are done by. Of the two legitimate approaches to training—the authoritarian versus the participative, it should be very obvious by now which one I prefer. I have criticized many of the arguments that are usually used to buttress the authoritarian approach. First, there is the mechanistic explanation of the aids. The holes in this theory were exposed in chapter 7. This explanation is often used to justify what I consider to be an over emphasis on the need for expert riding. If the aids did work automatically, then perfect position would be as important as most people believe it is. As it is, being able to explain to the horse what it is you want him to do is at least as important as riding him well. This is not to say that good riding is unimportant; but few of us are athletic enough to make great riders and I believe that anyone can train a horse. Authoritarians also usually claim that horses are so stupid that they must be guided solely by their brainy riders. In my opinion, horses can be called stupid only by those who fail to appreciate their point of view. Certainly any animal who is capable of learning the dressage communication system, as I have described it, is far from stupid. Horses may have their physical limits in dressage, but almost any horse can learn the language of the aids and acquire the right psychological attitudes towards being ridden. In my opinion, the best policy to follow is to become close friends with your horse, each of you perceiving the other as a unique individual. Establishing the necessary respect, trust, confidence, and understanding for this type of relationship does take a great deal of time and patience. However, anyone who tries it will discover the true joys of companionship with his horse.

Source Materials and Suggested Readings

Horse psychology is a subject upon which very little has been written. The only book available in English on this subject is the one by Moyra Williams. Her discussion of perception is especially valuable. Both of Young's books also contain much valuable advice on horse handling for an inexperienced trainer. Chapter 15 was strongly influenced by my own reading in ethology, the scientific study of animal behavior in the wild. Chapter 16 was based on ideas borrowed from the psychological study of the best ways to handle humans at work. Podhajsky's books probably come closest to expressing the ideal of participative management that I have been trying to describe. My own approach to horse management has been greatly influenced by the concepts of humanistic psychology.

PART VI

Planning a Training Program

18
Evaluating Progress

Now that the physical, linguistic, and psychological aspects of dressage schooling have been described separately, the time has come to put them back together and discuss designing a training program. One of the biggest problems a novice faces is establishing the right goals. The mistake most people make is to try to accomplish too much, too fast. Dressage training always takes a great deal of time. In defining objectives, the dressage tests can be very helpful. A reasonable goal for most amateurs is to try and advance one test level for each year of training. Of course, an experienced trainer can take a green colt through Stage 1 in a year; but a horse and rider team with no dressage experience usually have a lot to unlearn. This is also the stage at which the rider usually has to spend a great deal of time improving his position and learning how to use his aids effectively. This unlearning and relearning process is frustrating and discouraging. It is also time consuming. The average novice is better off if he plans on spending two years, instead of one, in passing through Stage 1.

The place to start program design is with a diagnostic analysis. First, take Table I and try to figure out what qualities you and your horse do or do not have. Second, take the tests and decide what exercises you can and cannot do. This should give you some idea as to what level you want to attempt to reach. Once the level has been decided, carefully analyze your strengths and weaknesses. The tests are written for an average horse. Each individual horse is usually ahead of the level requirements in some ways and behind in others. Once your weaknesses have been pinpointed, you can concentrate on correcting them. Let me give you two examples of this type of analysis. In both cases, the riders wanted to reach first level. Horse number one had a naturally calm disposition and was always perfectly relaxed. Unlike most horses, who have not had any dressage training, she was not at all stiff. She did accept the bit fairly well, although she found the use of combined aids rather puzzling. Her major problem was a complete lack of forward impulsion and engagement of the hindquarters. This was what needed correction. She had to learn to go forward at energetic working paces. Although she had not been correctly trained, she had not been spoiled and bringing her up to standard was not too difficult. This horse after some intensive and successful training is shown in Photograph 3a. Horse number two was a green Thoroughbred. He was stiff, badly balanced, and refused to accept contact. A lot of quiet work, particularly on circles, helped loosen him up. Work on transitions and lunging helped cure his balance problem. This horse, after nine months of patient training, is shown in Photograph 3b.

Since diagnostic analysis is usually somewhat beyond an inexperienced novice, he does need help. The ideal answer is regular lessons from a good, local instructor. Such teachers are rare, so this is not always possible and many people are forced to depend on an occasional show or clinic for guidance. The problems involved in interpreting test results will be discussed in Chapter 20. The rider should also make an attempt to talk to the judge or instructor personally. These people are generally very knowledgeable and they can be quite helpful. Those without a good local teacher can also try and help each other. A group of friends can get together regularly and ride dressage tests for each other. They can then practice scoring each other either on the standard test sheets or by using Table I. This table was worked out originally as an aid for just such friendly evaluation. The advantages to using this system will also be discussed in chapter 20. Learning dressage is never easy. The novice should study, think, observe, analyze, and reflect about his own horse and any others he can find to watch. The best way to learn is to never stop asking why, even if it does infuriate the experts at times.

There are three phases to learning dressage. First, the student has to understand each quality and exercise theoretically—its definition, value, and place in the training program. Hopefully this book has been helpful in defining the principles and objectives of training, as well as the casual relationships among qualities. The novice also needs to know exactly how much can be expected from a horse at each stage in training. The dressage tests and some of the material in this book should provide some guidance in this area. However, no one has ever learned to ride by reading a book. The next step is observation. The student needs to acquire a mind's eye picture of what the horse should look like when he is working correctly. Specific demonstrations and constant observations of horses at various stages of training are essential in acquiring these mental pictures. Attending shows and clinics can be invaluable in this process. Hopefully the photographs in this book have also been of assistance. Finally, the student has to acquire a kinesthetic impression of how the horse should feel under him when he is working correctly or incorrectly. Learning to interpret these feelings is the most difficult and critical part of dressage and it can be taught only by horses. An instructor can explain theory and provide demonstrations, but a rider must learn to interpret through experience. Even the most advanced dressage riders still need a coach on the ground to catch the inevitable errors.

One of the difficulties with most textbooks on training is that they tend to be overdogmatic. The reader is left with the impression that all he has to do is follow the author's method, using his magic formulas, and all will be well. This is misleading to say the least. There is no one way to train a horse. Even though there is general agreement on the overall objectives of dressage training, each rider or trainer is bound to emphasize different qualities and exercises. This produces an individual style. Different as my two horses are, they both very plainly bear a stamp which says that the same person trained them. Even when the objectives of training are the same, the ways of reaching them must differ with each horse. Horses are unique individuals, no two can be handled alike. Everyone encounters problems in training and there are no set ways, no rigid formulas for solving them. The experts have two great advantages. They are able to spot difficulties much sooner because they are able to interpret what they feel under them so much better. They also have their wide experience to guide them in trying various remedies. Diagnosing a problem is only the first step. The second one is finding the right solution for this particular horse. This may take a lot of time and many trials before the correct answer is found. At any point in training, consulting an expert is always worthwhile. They can help diagnose the problems and suggest possible solutions. Obtaining a regular evaluation of progress, either forwards or backwards, is an essential part of training.

19
Program Planning

After you have conducted a diagnostic analysis, the next step is to plan a training program. This program should include both long and short term goals. The eventual goal is to produce a well-schooled horse, who can show all of the qualities described in Table I. A more immediate goal is to progress one test level for each year of training. However, neither of these objectives is very helpful for day-to-day schooling. Short term goals are also needed. These are objectives which you can attempt to reach over the next few weeks or months. A diagnostic analysis that pinpoints your horse's weak spots is essential in establishing them. First, you may need to concentrate on cultivating certain qualities. Perhaps your horse is weak on lateral flexion and needs a lot of work on circles. Maybe he has a habit of resisting the bit and needs to be persuaded to accept correct contact. You must be aware of these faults and the reason why they exist. A problem may be physical, linguistic, or emotional in nature. Even after the cause of a problem has been discovered, a trainer still has to keep trying different remedies until he finds one that works. Second, at a particular stage in training, you may need to concentrate on mastering certain exercises. For example, I am now drilling one of my horses intensively on counter cantering and simple changes of lead as a preparation for flying changes. Once these goals have been established, each schooling session should be analyzed as to your progress in reaching them. To plan your next schooling session intelligently, you need to know where your horse is showing signs of improvement and where he seems to be encountering some difficulties. Admittedly, an experienced professional may not bother with this type of conscious planning, but the typical novice will generally accomplish very little without it.

Once the appropriate goals have been established, a suitable routine needs to be worked out. A pattern of activities which suits one horse and rider team, may not necessarily suit another. In my experience, three workouts a week is the absolute minimum for serious training. With an older horse this is barely adequate; but can be managed by working the horse hard at relatively infrequent intervals. However, a young horse has much less stamina, so he does need to be worked more often and much less strenuously. Personally I like to plan a rather varied program; I have found that horses tend to get bored quite quickly with just dressage work. Some relaxation outside of a ring can do wonders for a horse's attitude and performance. A few good runs can be a great relief after a lot of collection. My horses also know that as long as they obey rules 1 and 2, they are free to relax off contact. However, establishing the right pattern of activities can be a problem. I generally prefer to alternate between ring work and hacking, but such patterns do need to be adjusted to the individual. For example, with one of my horses I found that the optimal sequence seemed to be one session on basic dressage, followed by one on more advanced dressage, followed by a trail ride. Either the basic session or the trail ride occasionally included some easy jumping for variety's sake. My other horse tolerates much less ring work. I get the best results with him if I take him out once or twice for each session in the ring.

A planned program may be essential, but this does not mean that those plans do not frequently go awry. Everyone, horses and riders alike, can have an off day. The weather is also bound to interfere at times. What is really frustrating is that horses rarely improve at an even rate. There are always many exasperating plateaus in training when the horse seems to be making no forward progress at all. These will eventually be followed by sudden exciting leaps forward, which make up for the patience needed to survive the plateaus. Regardless of what progress you may or may not be making technically, there is one important principle which should never be overlooked. The horse must discover that attempting to please you does pay off and that noncooperation only leads to unpleasant consequences. My practice has always been that horses who behave are worked less hard, praised more, and allowed to spend more time on the activities which they enjoy the most. Uncooperative horses are worked harder, scolded more, and made to do all the things which they hate the most. Following this policy will eventually convince a horse that willing cooperation is the best course to follow.

Any schooling session is normally divided into three phases. In the first phase, the horse is warmed up so that serious work can begin. In the second and longest phase, the horse is gradually worked up to the best possible level of performance in the work which he already understands. Finally, on the horse's good days, a few minutes may be spent on new work. Any or all of these phases should be broken up by occasional rest periods at a free walk. Each schooling session should progress from the most elementary work to the most advanced work of which the horse is capable. Every session begins with the same goals; the horse must be on the bit, moving energetically forward, and relaxed before any advanced work can be undertaken. Of course, achieving these goals may take months of work with a young horse, while a trained horse can attain them in five minutes. However, the same pattern from elementary to advanced holds true, regardless of what stage of training the horse is in. The work which completes a session may vary tremendously in level of difficulty; the level at which it begins does not.

Within this general pattern there is room for a good deal of individual variation. This is particularly true of the warm-up period.

29. Any schooling session should be broken up by rest periods at a free walk. Chief shows how relaxing he finds the relief from working on contact.

The amount of time needed and the best exercises to use vary a good deal from horse to horse. They may even vary with the same horse, depending on the season of the year, the weather, and the mood he is in on that particular day. I don't believe that there is any one prescription for warming up that could possibly suit every horse. Each trainer has to experiment to find out what works best with each individual horse. For example, slow and sticky are the words which best describe the way in which one of my horses normally begins a schooling session. I have learned from experience to just let him trot or canter quietly for about 15 minutes at the beginning of every session. Until he has loosened up and started to move out of his own free will, there is no point in pushing him or asking him to execute any difficult exercises. My other horse is just the opposite. Instead of being lethargic, she usually starts out with a burst of energy. It usually takes a few minutes of lively trotting or cantering to get her to settle down and attend to anything besides a desire to run. The fact that one horse starts out lazy, the other explosive, is something to which I, as their trainer, have to adjust.

In the second phase there is also a good deal of variation, depending on the stage of training, the diagnostic analysis, and the horse's daily variations in mood and condition. Intelligent planning is of critical importance in this phase. The long term goals determine in general what exercises are to be used and what level of performance is to be expected. The short term goals, established through diagnostic analysis, control the specific objectives. In phase 2 the trainer must concentrate on those exercises which cultivate the qualities which the horse lacks at the moment. For example, I have been using all winter varying combinations of exercises in an attempt to get more impulsion into my horses' collected paces. The whole idea of a schooling session is to expose the horse's problems and to work on their cure. It is this endless polishing of known exercises which teaches a horse the habit of obedience and lays the foundation for improved performance.

Day-to-day variations in how the horse happens to be feeling also affect the activities that are carried on in phase 2. The short and long term goals represent an over-all plan, but there are also problems which show up in each individual session. In my experience, there seem to be three basic factors that vary from day to day. The horse may be feeling stiff or supple, lazy or energetic, and cooperative or noncooperative. The immediate goal in every session is to overcome whatever the horse appears to lack on that particular day. The length of a session will frequently vary, depending on which of these problems shows up in the course of the work-out. For example, extra suppling exercises may have to be introduced or a noncooperative horse may have to be worked until he gives in and starts to obey willingly. Good days are days to quit early; bad days are days to work the horse extra hard. Eventually the horse should learn that the sooner he works well, the sooner he will get to stop work for the day.

Basically what has occurred in phase 2 will determine if the horse ever gets to phase 3 on a particular day. Some schooling sessions are always much more successful than others. Only when the horse is working well up to his current performance level, can the trainer afford to proceed to new work. This is, by definition, work that the horse still finds difficult, demanding, and probably painful. On bad days, phase 3 is never reached at all; on exceptionally good days, it will be reached sooner than usual. This phase is always short. First, the horse should be asked to do whatever he currently finds most difficult. Then, the second he shows any signs of an acceptable response, work should stop for the day. This is a trainer's most powerful reward and it should be used with great care. It is, for example, always used to teach the horse the meaning of a new command. A session should always end on a high note. The horse should learn that all he has to do is to willingly tackle something horribly difficult and then no more will be asked of him.

Just how long a normal schooling session should be is not an easy question to answer. A great deal depends on the horse's age, general physical condition, and fitness. It is actually more important to consider how strenuously a horse is worked than how long he is worked. I find that I can work a horse harder in 30 minutes of dressage than I can in several hours of cross-country work. In my opinion, an hour is usually more than enough for something as demanding as dressage. The horse should never be worked until he is either mentally bored or physically exhausted. The more willing a horse is, the more careful you should be about how much you ask of him. By observing how your horse acts, both before and after his workout, you should be able to tell if your program has been too strenuous for him. Horses do communicate their feelings with their whole bodies. Any serious trainer is well advised to learn to understand their body language. How a horse greets you can indicate whether or not he is looking forward to working. Lethargy, depression, or unfriendliness after work usually indicates that he has been pushed too hard. Observing where the horse has sweated can also give you helpful information as to which muscles you have succeeded in flexing. Horsemanship is more than just riding a horse, it is also observing and handling him on the ground.

30. *Observation on the ground can tell you a great deal about the horse's reaction to your training program.*

30a. Chief is alertly watching me approach with the saddle, curious as to what interesting activities I have planned for the day.

30b. An affectionate moment after work.

After all that has been said about program design, there is very little left to be said about preparing for a dressage test. Riding a test should simply represent the last 6 or 7 minutes of your normal schooling session. This is, of course, the new work period or phase 3. There is only one major difference between riding in competition and schooling. In training, you pull out and work on your problems; in competition, you attempt to cover them up. However, a horse should never be expected to go as well at a show as he does at home. Almost everyone is nervous at a show and this tension always communicates itself to the horse. The best policy is usually to show the horse somewhat below his current level of competence at home. You should normally be well prepared for a test at least three months before a show. This will then give you plenty of time to polish the specific exercises and transitions in the test. However, polishing does not mean that you should keep riding the test over and over. That is disastrous because the horse soon learns its pattern. What you should do is analyze the test so that you can invent different patterns and combinations of the exercises and transitions. These should then be worked into your normal schooling sessions. Finally, there is no need to take the show results too seriously. Even if you win, there is undoubtedly still plenty of room for improvement. If you get a low score, you should still remember that your horse did his best.

20
The Irrational Aspects of Competitive Dressage

Rather obviously by now, I find it impossible to take dressage competitions very seriously. My reasons for this are based on the irrational aspects of the scoring system used in judging them. In my opinion, this system helps turn competitive dressage into a social game that can be taken seriously only by those interested in achieving status through winning prizes. Personally I see dressage as a partnership between horse and rider for the purpose of mutual self-development. Unfortunately judging, under the present system, tends to encourage the snobbish and game aspects of dressage. Certainly this system rarely produces either educational or objective results. The mere use of numbers can do nothing to improve the quality of biased judgments. Mathematical computations alone cannot produce accurate or reliable results. Most of the people involved in competitive dressage seem to have an almost mystical faith in the value of the present system. Believe it or not, this system was not handed down by God, but developed by fallible humans. These people may have been experts in dressage, but they obviously knew very little about designing rating scales to produce consistent and valid results. The system they developed gives free rein to irrational prejudices, leads to biased observations, and creates ill feeling at practically every show.

Before reliable judgments can be obtained, three conditions must be met. First, standardized criteria must be developed. Second, the relative emphasis to be placed on each criterion must be specified. Third, judges must be trained to interpret these standards in the same way. In dressage, we do have standardized test patterns, but that is about all. Judges may even disagree on how an exercise, such as the shoulder-in, should be executed. There is even less agreement on the meaning of a complex quality, such as impulsion. Authority has laid down what a horse can be expected to do at the various test levels, but failed to clearly specify how it should be done. The real problem is the lack of definition as to what constitutes correctness at each individual test level. A good movement at one level may be very different from a good movement at another level. Until some of these theoretical problems are worked out, there is going to be no way to obtain consistent judgments in dressage competitions. Now, two judges can, and often do, differ by as much as 50% in scoring the same horse. What one judge may consider good, another judge may consider bad. This kind of inconsistency is both baffling and infuriating for a rider who tries to take his test results seriously. If he does not know what criteria the judge is using to judge him by, he has no way to interpret the scores and comments he receives. Until good evaluative standards are developed, competitive dressage will remain a noneducational experience.

Aside from the lack of standards, there is one other basic flaw in the present system. There is never any point in a dressage test at which the judge is actually scoring one thing at a time. Tests are separated into two parts—scores for individual movements and general impressions. Scores are assigned for general impressions towards the end of a performance, individual scores as it proceeds. A novice usually assumes that the individual scores will be based on whether or not he and his horse did the right thing at the right moment. This is not the case. At each moment, they are also being judged on a whole range of qualities, from impulsion to relaxation. Since no human could possibly assign and average 20 scores in 30 seconds, what a judge usually does is take a general impression as the horse enters the ring. He decides at this point that this is a 4 horse or a 7 horse in general quality. He then varies his scores by 1 or 2 points depending on how well the movements are actually executed. This is why a horse who commits a major disobedience may still receive a higher score than one who actually does what he is supposed to. This approach to judging naturally tends to maximize, rather than minimize, the impact of the judge's prejudices on the scores he assigns. In essence, a judge is prejudging the horse and rider before they have actually had a chance to perform.

In scoring general impression, composite scores are still the rule. The horse is given three scores—the first for regularity and freedom of paces, the second for impulsion, and the third for obedience, lightness, and suppleness. In assigning all three scores, the emphasis is usually placed on physical qualities, rather than on the horse's psychological attitudes or linguistic competence. In regard to the first score, I have yet to see a clear definition of free paces. This term is apparently used to indicate how far the horse is reaching out from his shoulder as he moves. This quality, of course, is completely dependent on the horse's conformation and the degree to which he is engaging his hindquarters. Regularity is the quality of rhythm, but it is always strongly influenced by relaxation and impulsion. Impulsion, as I explained in chap. 5, is actually controlled by conformation, engagement of the hindquarters, and the amount of energy being expended in moving forward. There is no reason why suppleness and obedience should be scored together, one is a physical quality and the other a psychological one. A stiff horse may very well still be doing his best to obey, while a supple horse can be thoroughly disobedient. Even if these two qualities are scored separately, they still represent composite scores. A horse may flex well on some movements and poorly on others. He may disobey out of fear, misunderstanding, or willfulness. Scoring lightness along with obedience and suppleness only compounds the problem. All of the physical qualities affect lightness, especially the horse's ability to collect. By now it should be obvious that at no point in a dressage test is it ever clear exactly what the judge is supposed to be evaluating. This lack of clarity gives a judge a great deal of freedom to emphasize whatever he wills. The result, of course, is that no two judges ever score alike.

There are two options in developing an evaluative measure. One choice is to assign one score for the entire performance. This system gives the most consistent results and is the best one if competition is the sole objective. The other choice is to assign one score to each quality that can affect the overall result. This system is much better from the educational viewpoint since it should point the performer's strong and weak points. However, it is much more difficult to use effectively. To get good results with such a system, two things are essential. First, the performance must be analyzed until all of the relevant qualities are identified and isolated for scoring. Second, weights must be assigned, indicating the relative importance of each quality. The system that is currently being used in competitive dressage represents an attempt to develop the second kind of system. Unfortunately, in this case, the necessary analysis has never been carried far enough. The dressage system lacks clearly defined criteria and uses composite scores. These limitations destroy most of its potential educational value. There seems to be a good deal of dissatisfaction with this system. However, most people tend to blame the judges, instead of looking for flaws in the system. The way it is set up now, there is no way in which consistent, objective results could be regularly obtained from it. Some of the best judges do, of course, manage to transcend the limitations of the system.

Since the current system is so inadequate, I was forced to search for something better. I did want to find an evaluative system for this book that could be a helpful guide for ·an inexperienced trainer. The result of my search was Table I. Using the current tests as a starting point, I tried out different lists of qualities until I found one that gave me one score for each quality I thought important. I then worked out some very careful definitions as to exactly what could be expected from the horse at each level. If each of these nine qualities (engagement of the hindquarters, suppleness, regularity of paces, obedience to the leg aids, acceptance of contact, smoothness and precision of transitions, relaxation, attentiveness, willingness) is scored individually, I found that a very educational pattern appeared. This worked very well for Stage 1 horses. For Stage 2 horses, individual movements may need to be scored for correct execution. These scores can then be averaged, if necessary, to produce a general score for suppleness. Three sample score sheets are shown in Table V. They are illustrations of how this evaluative measure can be put into practice. In scoring, I do use the conventional 10-point scale. However, I interpret the numbers differently. Instead of the absolute scale used in the current tests, I use an open-ended one. Both scales are also shown in Table I. An open-ended scale, in my opinion, is much better since it clearly indicates that standards do change with the test level.

In contrast to the current competitive system, the one I developed does seem to produce helpful results. There are several reasons for this. It is simple to use, based on clearly defined criteria, and easy for the nonexpert to understand and apply. Along with abandoning composite scores, it also gives the judge more time to analyze the horse's problems and to make helpful comments. Despite these advantages, I am not necessarily advocating a change in the existing system. This would probably require an act of God. However, my system could be used either in clinics or among friends who are trying to help each other. Its major function was meant to be educational, rather than competitive. It does, I admit, reveal my personal prejudices. I have given the physical, linguistic, and psychological qualities equal weight; instead of emphasizing the physical ones as the current tests do. This is because I feel that they are all equally important in producing a pleasant horse to ride. The physical ones are, of course, much more important if a flashy performance is the main objective. In my experience, no judge has ever commented on how happy the horse looks and this is something which concerns me very much.

By now, the two basic flaws in the present judging system should be very apparent. First, composite scores are used. This means that the judge's criteria are never defined for the exhibitor. It also means that the judge is allowed to weight or emphasize any qualities he pleases. Second, there is very little agreement as to what criteria are to be used in judging a horse at different points in training. Horses in the lower levels are all too often judged for potential than on performance. Of course, some standards do exist and are described in

Table V, Sample Evaluation Sheets

Marking Scale (Used in current tests)

10 Excellent
9 Very Good
8 Good
7 Fairly Good
6 Satisfactory
5 Sufficient
4 Insufficient
3 Fairly Bad
2 Bad
1 Very Bad

Open-ended Scale (Used on sheets below)

9-10 Too good, horse should move to higher level
7-8 Excellent for this level
5-6 Adequate for this level
3-4 Below standard for this level
1-2 Way below standard, horse does not belong on this level

Sample 1 (Training Level)

Engagement of the Hindquarters	— 3	Horse not being driven up to bit
Suppleness	— 5	
Regularity of Paces	— 6	
Obedience to the Leg Aids	— 3	Rider too passive, horse not moving out
Acceptance of Contact	— 6	
Smoothness and Precision of Transitions	— 8	Exceptionally accurate & smooth
Relaxation	— 9	Horse too calm
Attentiveness	— 3	Horse half-asleep
Willingness	— 4	Horse obedient, but lazy

Sample 2 (1st level)

Engagement of the Hindquarters	— 5	Horse still showing some stiffness in back and neck, resisting contact

Suppleness	— 4	Horse is not relaxed, therefore shows no signs of developing suppleness
Regularity of Paces	— 2	Horse restless, constant tempo changes, he is being upset by rider
Obedience to the Leg Aids	— 6	Horse is driving forward
Acceptance of Contact	— 2	Horse consistently above bit
Smoothness and Precision of Transitions	— 2	Rough, rider's hands too hard, forcing accuracy too soon
Relaxation	— 2	Rider upsetting horse, asking for more with legs, than can accept with hands
Attentiveness	— 5	Horse obviously being trained by force, not patience
Willingness	— 4	Horse must be calmed down, both he and rider must learn to relax

Sample 3 (3rd level)

Engagement of the Hindquarters	— 3	Insufficient collection
Suppleness	— 4.9	See below
Regularity of Paces	— 6	Very even, lacks impulsion
Obedience to the Leg Aids	— 4	Lacks energy
Acceptance of Contact	— 9	Absolutely reliable, no resistance
Smoothness and Precision of Transitions	— 8	Very fluid and precise
Relaxation	— 9	Horse completely relaxed
Attentiveness	— 9	
Willingness	— 9	Horse not quite up to test requirements, but obviously giving all she has to give

Gait Transitions	— 7	Horse should take fewer steps in canter-walk transitions
Pace Transitions	— 4	Not defined enough, extension would improve with more collection
Circles	— 3	Either too large or right size and horse lost impulsion
Shoulder-in	— 3	Some signs of correct flexion to right
Pivots	— 5	Smooth, but could be done with fewer steps
Counter-canter	— 6	Flexion correct, horse tends to rush a little on right lead
Rein-back	— 5	Horse should be taking longer steps

Note: The current tests do include a fourth score under general impressions. This is a composite score judging the rider's position and correct use of the aids. Since this book is concerned with the training of the horse, I ignored this score in working out an evaluative system. However, if the rider's horsemanship is to be judged, I have found it best to use three scores—one for position, one for use of the leg aids, and one for use of the hand aids.

Notes on Dressage. Unfortunately, they are expressed in highly technical language. They are also based on an attempt to define absolute standards, rather than relative ones. They might suit the purposes of high school dressage, but not the needs of the novice. What we need is a standard for each test level that clearly specifies what level of performance is to be expected from the horse. In particular, the relative seriousness of various kinds of errors does need to be established. Something, which may be overlooked at one level, may be critically important at a more advanced level. Many people feel that a first level test is as difficult to ride perfectly as a third level test. In my opinion, this assumption is incorrect. If a horse could do a first level test perfectly, he should not be competing on that level. A Stage 1 horse does not look like an advanced horse and he should not be expected to do so. Two levels of performance are involved, not one. In the same sense, sixth graders and college students are not expected to produce themes of the same quality.

The attempt to develop an absolute standard is, I believe, based on a misconception about the very nature of dressage. It is an art, not a science. The only quality that can be measured accurately is precision. The other qualities can only be approached by opinionated guesses or estimates. Assigning numbers to such guesses does nothing to improve their objectivity. They are always going to be biased by the personal prejudices of the people who make them. There are always going to be different schools of thought in dressage, as well as individual preferences. This means that it will never be possible to achieve consensus. Everyone has a somewhat different concept of what constitutes a well-trained horse. This concept then influences the emphasis placed on different qualities and exercises. Such diversity of opinion is what makes dressage an art. It is also what makes the development of clear criteria and established standards so important in judging. If a final consensus could be reached, then the artistic elements of dressage would be destroyed forever. However, before educational communication can take place, some degree of standardization is essential. These standards, of course, should not be treated as the final word. They will simply represent the most popular opinions of the moment.

Many of the people who support the current competitive system are engaged in fooling themselves. They may claim that they are engaging in an educational enterprise for the benefit of the horse, but what they are really doing is playing a social game. This game can be successfully played only by those who know the right terminology and follow the current fashions. Two aspects of the judging system encourage this game. One is the lack of clear criteria and the other is the use of composite scores. Most competitors eventually learn to give the judges the right kind of performance, but only after a good deal of expensive and frustrating experience. The right performance is, of course, defined by standards that are never made explicit. To define them logically in simple language might reveal their irrational nature. For those who play the show game, fashion is often much more important than horsemanship. The horse's education is supposed to be judged in the dressage ring, not his breed or dress. What he or his rider are wearing has very little to do with their performance. A review of the history of dressage quickly reveals how often fashions have changed in these matters. Anyone can do dressage. An English saddle, hunt attire, and an expensive horse are not essential. Adherence to such conventions may be required for winning, but not for training.

To show or not to show is a personal decision. Anyone who wishes to take the show game seriously must invest a good deal of money in the right type of horse, clothes, and equipment. There are, however, reasons for showing that do not relate to winning. Moving up one test a year represents an excellent training goal. Showing is good experience for a green horse. Going away from home and learning to concentrate in strange surroundings should be part of any horse's training. Shows are also excellent places to observe many horses in different stages of training. However, the novice should never let himself be fooled by the fact that test scores are computed mathematically. They still represent biased observations, made by biased humans using a biased system. Show results should never be taken too seriously and always viewed with a certain degree of cynicism.

21
My Equine Partners

After so much discussion on the principles and practice of dressage schooling, the time has finally come to discuss my two co-authors more fully. These co-authors are, of course, my two horses—Chief Reason and Gay Sprite. In a very real sense, this book simply represents an attempt to clarify, organize, and articulate what I have learned from years of working with them. They know, as no one else could, how many stupid mistakes I have made and what a mediocre rider I am, yet they still do their best to please me. In my experience, learning is always a matter of making mistakes, correcting them, and making more mistakes. This is certainly a perfect description of our struggles with dressage. Novice trainers are just as bound to make mistakes as green horses are to encounter problems. Errors, discouraging as they may be, are a fundamental part of education. One of the reasons why dressage interests me so much is that you never run out of things to work on; there is always some place to go. My horses still manage to teach me something new every time I work with them.

Like so many dedicated horrsemen, I have spent most of my spare time and cash on horses ever since I can remember. Over the years, I have ridden many horses and observed hundreds more—both well and badly trained and well and badly ridden. Chief and Gay feature in this book only because I have trained them both myself from the time they were barely broken. Merely riding does not necessarily teach anything about horse handling; attempting to school certainly does. To me the true test of horsemanship is being able to take a green colt and turn him into a well-behaved, reliable horse who is a pleasure to ride. I have always looked at a young horse as clay, to be shaped for good or ill in his trainer's hands. Success in this process seems to depend far more on patience, tact, and determination than on riding skill. As some of the photographs in this book illustrate, I am far from being a first class rider, yet Chief and Gay are living testimonials to what I have been able to accomplish as a trainer. Admittedly my poor balance often limits the performance level we could reach together, but this really doesn't seem to bother the horses. Success in the show ring may demand expert riding and quality horses; creating pleasant riding horses does not.

My interest in dressage dates back a long time, but Chief was the one who really convinced me that it was worth-while. I bought him ten years ago as a green broke four year old, two weeks off the Montana range. He was originally trained as most hunters are, becoming a decent hack and a very reliable jumper. Seven years ago we took up dressage under the guidance of a knowledgeable instructor. After several years the difference in the horse was almost unbelievable. His whole appearance and way of going had changed. I now had a supple, springy horse to ride, instead of a stiff, badly balanced one. What pleased me the most was that he had become so much more responsive. He could now be ridden on a snaffle and controlled with a touch, even when being menaced by dangerous dragons.

Chief was also the one who helped me discover that showing and hunting were not what I really wanted to do. I found that what I valued the most was something I had had all along. This was the friendship, the emotional rapport, between us. He convinced me that dressage competitions are just as artificial a test of a well-trained horse, as hunter classes are of field hunters. Every expert for whom I have ever ridden, as a judge or instructor, has made approximately the same comment about him. They say that he is a nice horse and obviously well trained, but why am I wasting so much time and money on such a mediocre animal? They overlook two major points in this general opinion. One, Chief is a "nice" horse because of the way he has been handled. Two, I don't judge a horse by his appearance any more than I do a human. I think so highly of Chief because of the way he treats me, works for me, and takes care of me. He not only frequently does the impossible for me, he is also firmly convinced that it is his job to keep me on his back. What counts, in my opinion, is how hard a horse tries to please you, not what performance level he is able to achieve.

Of course, neither Chief nor I found dressage easy. I find it hard to imagine that anyone could ever encounter more serious problems than we did. He was stiff as a board, down on his forehand, and had a mouth like steel. I rode too far forward, hung on one side of the

31. A horse and a human can find a great deal of pleasure in each other's company.

31a. Chief is carefully surveying the countryside for dragons. He considers it his job to take care of himself and me too.

31b. An exchange of compliments. Chief is insinuating that it is about time he got some attention too.

31c. The four friends, equine and human, enjoying each other's company cross country.

horse, and had no idea of how to use my aids correctly. Both of us found the process of improvement to be an extremely painful one. The only thing that saved us was his good nature and my determination. I give him most of the credit for our accomplishments. He did all of the work, in response to my inept explanations. All I really did was to struggle very hard to improve my riding so as to help him. He has now been a competent 3rd level horse for several years and I have discovered what a joy riding a trained horse can be.

When I decided to buy another horse four years ago, I tried to find one as different from Chief as possible. My success with him might have been accidental, so I wanted to see if my ideas on training would work as well with an entirely different type of horse. My search was successful; Gay is as different from Chief as two horses can be. In conformation, temperament, and experience, they are complete opposites. Of course, Chief had to be reschooled; Gay was relatively unspoiled. The main problems I encountered with Chief were physical; with Gay they were emotional. She had never had to obey anyone; Chief had learned to trust, respect, and cooperate with me before we even started working on dressage. I sometimes wonder if it matters what you teach a horse, so long as you work with him on something and learn to understand each other in the process. The main advantage of dressage is, of course, the amount of time involved in training; as well as the gymnastic and linguistic side benefits.

Nothing distinguishes my two horses more than their attitude towards people. Chief apparently was brutally broken and to this day he refuses to trust anyone except me. He has always been an exceptionally bold horse; the only thing he has ever really been afraid of is people. Gay is just the opposite. She is exceptionally cowardly, even for a horse. The only thing she has never been afraid of is people. Chief is suspicious of strangers, Gay regards them as potential admirers. Her emotional problems in training were caused by a combination of vanity, willfulness, and fear. She thought that she was so beautiful and charming that there was no reason why she should have to work for a living, much less do anything that she didn't happen to want to do. Convincing her otherwise was an exhausting process. Unlike Chief, she encountered very little physical pain in training, but she did experience a great deal of outrage and fear. We accomplished very little in our first two years together, but once she had learned to trust and respect me, she started making rapid strides forward. She is now working into third level and has become a very pleasant ride.

The emphasis I have put on patience, sympathy, and kindness in training does not mean that there are not times when you have to get tough with a horse. A horse has to learn to respect his rider, otherwise he is going to see no reason to obey him. My worst battles with Gay were over cross-country hazards. She was simply terrified of the outside world. We had some nasty fights before she learned it was safe to go any place I asked. On the other hand, Chief tended to get stubborn about what he thought were unreasonable demands in the ring. Serious disagreements, however, should be quite rare. For example, in the five years during which I worked regularly with an instructor, I can remember only three occasions when he told me that what my horse needed was discipline. Otherwise, all of our problems had been caused by my ignorance or poor riding. There is no point in starting a fight when the rider, not the horse, is at fault.

Now, after years of work, I have created two horses who are great fun to ride. The results have made the cost in time, agony, and effort well worthwhile. As their photographs show they are relaxed, willing, and responsive in many circumstances. Whether collected or uncollected, there is never any sense of constraint in their appearance.

32. Heading home, as the day's work is almost over.

They work freely, readily establishing contact with the bit without any signs of overflexing. They demonstrate the fact that you need neither an expensive nor a special horse to be able to do dressage. Of course, neither of my horses has had any outstanding success in the show ring, but I don't regard this as any real measure of the quality of their training. I look on ribbons and trophies as tinsel toys for children, my horses' opinions are more important to me than those of a judge. This is not to say I am against showing. Many people enjoy it, but I have ceased to find it rewarding. My horses and I enjoy our association with each other and continue to improve our understanding every time we see each other. This is what counts as far as I am concerned. Our technical proficiency may be questioned, but not our harmonious relationship.

Source Materials and Suggested Readings

For those who are keeping young horses at home, Young's books make some excellent suggestions on training programs. The last chapter in Wynmalen's *Dressage* discusses riding a dressage test, both from the competitor's and the judge's point of view. William's *Adventures Unbridled* and Podhajsky's *My Horses, My Teachers* both contain some fascinating accounts of training problems and their resolution.

A Final Word

Before ending, I do have a few final comments to make. First, I must admit that I have probably learned more from writing this book than anyone else could from reading it. In horsemanship, as in any other subject, the more you learn, the more there is to know. Unfortunately the value, application, and interpretation of dressage are all controversial subjects. However, despite all the disputes, there still is a common body of theoretical knowledge. I tried to make very clear distinctions between general principles, controversial points, and my own opinions. If this book has made any major contribution to theory, it has been in the clarification of the interwoven objectives of dressage and in the scientific analysis of the language of the aids. Within this framework of theory, there is room for a good deal of variation and individual emphasis. Certainly each horse has his own problems and talents. Rather obviously by now, my own emphasis is on riding for fun and I value very highly the emotional rapport with my horses. I regard the gymnastic and linguistic techniques of dressage simply as the best means for achieving maximum enjoyment and fusion. In competitive dressage the emphasis is just the opposite. There it is on obtaining brilliant and spectacular movements. Unfortunately few of us can have the time, talent, and money which are so essential to achieving this quality of performance. However, anyone can use dressage as a means for improving his own horsemanship and making his horse a better ride. I only hope that some of you can begin to discover with your horse the same joy and companionship I have found with mine.

Appendix A—Summary of Test Requirements

The qualities a dressage horse is expected to show at different levels were summarized in Table I. They have also been extensively discussed throughout the book. The gymnastic exercises were described in Part 4. The specific test requirements, based on the 1971 American tests, are listed below. Copiet of the current tests may be obtained from the American Horse Show Association. Training practice, of course, should never be limited to just these patterns and precise exercises.

At training Level the horse is expected to show:
1. A working trot and canter.
   An ordinary walk (this just means a walk on contact as opposed to a free walk) and a free walk.
2. 66-ft. circles at a trot and canter.
3. Halt from a walk or trot, walk or trot from a halt, walk from a trot, trot from a walk, trot from a canter, canter from a trot on correct lead.

At first Level the horse is expected to show in addition:
1. A mild degree of extension at a trot.
2. 33-ft. circles at a trot.
3. Simple changes of lead through a trot.

At second Level the horse is expected to show in addition:
1. 26-ft. circles at a trot, 33-ft. circles at a canter.
2. Rein-back, pivot on the hindquarters, shoulder-in.

At third Level the horse is expected to show in addition:
1. Collected, ordinary, and extended paces at a trot and canter.
   An extended walk.
2. 20-ft. circles (voltes) at a trot, 26-ft. circles at a canter.
3. Walk or halt from canter, canter from walk or halt.
4. Simple changes of lead through a walk.
5. Counter cantering, two tracking (half pass) at a trot.

Appendix B—Sample Sentences

As in Table C, C will be used to stand for Combination. The place letters refer to the conventional dressage arena shown in Fig. 1.

Sample 1, introducing the horse to the pivot on the hindquarters:

The horse is on the right hand, proceeding at a walk in Position Straight. The rider uses C2 to bring him to a square halt. Two reduplications are required. The rider puts him into Position Right (°*), then applies moderate pressure with his left leg (L). This C4A. The horse backs up. The rider immediately drives him forward again with C1, returning to Position Straight in the process. The rider allows the horse to walk forward a few steps, then uses C2 three times to bring him to a halt again. C4A is repeated. This time the horse steps forward. The rider brings him to a halt again with one application of C2. C4A is repeated. This time the horse moves his hindquarters to the right. The rider, maintaining the halt (**), forcefully applies his right leg (L) to bring the horse's hindquarters back on the track. After a short pause, the rider again applies C4A. This time the horse takes two awkward steps to the right, attempting to pivot correctly. The rider immediately uses C2 to tell him to go straight forward, allowing him to go off contact as he moves out.

Sample 2, executing a figure eight at a canter:

The horse is cantering on the left lead. He is on the rail, flexed slightly to the inside. As he approaches E, the rider uses C5B; first asking for more position (*°) and then using his leg aids (L L) to ask for a 90-degree turn. As the horse approaches X, the rider reapplies his leg aids, asking for a circle. The horse takes too large a circle, so the rider asks for more flexion by shortening his inside rein and reapplying his leg aids, accentuating his outside leg. The horse then takes a circle of the desired size. As the horse approaches X again, the rider puts him into Position Straight and uses C2 twice to obtain a walk. After the horse has settled into a walk, the rider then asks him for a canter on the right lead. First he puts him into Position Right (°*), then he applies his leg aids (L   L), and gives slightly with both hands (°°). As the horse takes his first canter step, the rider reapplies his leg aids, asking for a circle right. This time the horse takes the right-sized circle, but allows his hindquarters to fall out. The rider firmly applies his outside leg, maintaining the pressure until the circle is completed. As the horse approaches X again, the rider uses both legs in Position 1 to tell him to go straight. As the horse approaches B, the rider drops his outside leg back again and applies his leg aids (L   L) to tell the horse to turn. As the horse finishes the 90-degree turn, the rider reduces the Position Right slightly, and lightly uses C1 to tell the horse to go straight forward.

Bibliography

Beudant, E. *Horse Training: Outdoor and High School.* New York: Charles Scribner's Sons, 1931.

Littauer, Vladimir S. *Common Sense Horsemanship,* 2nd ed. New York: Van Nostrand-Reinhold, 1963.

Littauer, Vladimir S. *Schooling Your Horse.* New York: Van Nostrand-Reinhold, 1956.

Podhajsky, Alois. *Complete Training of Horse and Rider in the Principles of Classical Horsemanship.* New York: Doubleday, 1967.

Podhajsky, Alois. *My Horses, My Teachers.* New York: Doubleday, 1968.

Seunig, Waldemar. *Horsemanship.* New York: Doubleday, 1961.

Williams, Moyra. *Adventures Unbridled.* New York: A. S. Barnes & Co., 1960.

Williams, Moyra. *Horse Psychology.* New York: A. S. Barnes & Co., 1957.

Wynmalen, Henry. *Dressage.* New York: A. S. Barnes, 1954.

Wynmalen, Henry. *Horse in Action.* New York: Van Nostrand-Reinhold, 1954.

Young, John Richard. *Schooling for Young Riders.* Norman, Oklahoma: University of Oklahoma Press, 1970.

Young, John Richard. *Schooling of the Western Horse.* Norman, Oklahoma: University of Oklahoma Press, 1954.

Index